ISBN: 0 9552876 0 X

Publisher's note

Formerly presented by Geoffrey Jones as a paper to the 2005 R&RTHA Annual Symposium

Edited by David Lowe FCILT

This edition published in 2006 by the Roads and Road Transport History Association Limited

Founded in 1992 to support historical research

Supported by the Department for Transport and the Freight Transport Association

Contents

Foreword by the Minister of State

In 1931 the first Traffic Commissioners were appointed and their initial duties included the administration and organisation of traffic, which primarily meant regulating bus operators and issuing licences. The 75th anniversary of Traffic Commissioners provides a welcome opportunity to look back at their valuable work and changing role over the years.

This book illustrates the significant changes that have occurred in the road haulage and passenger transport industries. The duties of the Traffic Commissioners have also been through a number of changes over this period. They now have a range of responsibilities including the licensing of operators of goods vehicles and of buses and coaches.

I welcome the publication of this material and I am sure that anyone with an interest in the history and regulation of the transport industry will also appreciate the efforts of those involved in its production. I hope this document will also lead to a wider audience appreciating the contribution made by Traffic Commissioners over the last 75 years.

Stephen Ladyman
Minister of State for Transport

Biography – Geoffrey Jones LLB

Geoffrey Jones was awarded an LL.B at Bristol University in 1959 and was admitted a solicitor in November 1962. He was a Lecturer at the College of Law, Guildford, from August 1962 until December 1963. He joined Cartwright Taylor & Corpe in Bristol in December 1963 (this firm eventually changing to Cartwrights).

In 1968 he became a partner and eventually senior partner until the firm's merger with Bond Pearce on 1 July 2001. Geoffrey first appeared in the traffic courts in 1967/8, appearing before Samuel Gibbon, Ronald Jackson and Major-General Elmslie. Eventually, he appeared in all Traffic Areas with the exception of Scotland.

On the retirement of Thomas Denner Corpe in 1972, Geoffrey took over responsibility for that side [transport] of the firm's practice and until he retired in April 2004.

Introduction

Over the last 75 years Traffic Commissioners have been amongst the most powerful individuals in the United Kingdom, representing prosecutor or inquisitor, judge, jury and executioner to the passenger and goods road transport industries and yet it is probably true to say that the public at large have never heard of them or, if they have, with very little concept of their history, powers and duties. Within the industry, almost without exception, they have been regarded with respect and frequently with affection. That can be said of very few regulators and it says a lot about the Commissioners themselves and the industries as a whole.

Notes:

For convenience in this text, the term Traffic Commissioner(s) is used interchangeably for the original full-time appointment of Chairman of the Traffic Commissioners, the Licensing Authority, the Licensing Authority for Public Service Vehicles/Goods Vehicles and the current position of Traffic Commissioner.

The items in italics in the following text are verbatim comments taken from the Annual Reports of the Traffic Commissioners.

1 Whence and why Traffic Commissioners?

Before the First World War urban passenger transport depended primarily on the horse-drawn omnibus and the electric tram. For into town and inter-urban public transport the comprehensive rail network provided the principal facility. The motor omnibus and the motor charabanc were just coming on the scene for urban and inter-urban transport. For example, whilst in the Cardiff area motor omnibuses were operating by 1907, they were not allowed to run into the City until 1910, while horse buses had continued to run until 1909[1]. In Bristol the first motor omnibus service was commenced by the Tramway Company on 17 January 1906 but there were only 12 such vehicles by 1912. Not until 1909 had it run its first charabanc tour to Wells and Cheddar.

From 1919 onwards there was a huge expansion in the use of motor omnibuses on both urban and inter-urban services and the development of longer distance 'coach' services[2]. On 22 July 1920 The Times reported:

> *'The immense and sudden increase in motor char-a-bancs traffic has its evil aspects. Not least of them is the behaviour of some of those persons who make a day's outing, generally on a Sunday, in one of these vehicles and are unable to remember that they are not the only people for whom the Sabbath were made.... This rowdyism can do nothing but serious harm to the young and rapidly growing road transport industry, and the Motor Trade Association has already met and discussed means of suppressing it.'*

A comparable explosion occurred in the use of motor lorries:

> *The problems ... stem from the enormous growth of road haulage after the war of 1914-1918. Motor transport had, of course, been extensively used during the war and many ex-servicemen commenced haulage on their own account afterwards. Many of them were owner/drivers doing not only driving but also*

maintenance repairs and clerical work. The results of this expansion were twofold. First, the abundance of road transport tended to result in the use of road haulage for long-distance through traffic in preference to rail because it was cheaper and more able to offer such a service at short notice. Secondly, in the road haulage industry itself there was keen and sometimes uneconomic competition which tended to result in inadequate maintenance and the over working of drivers, particularly on long distance services[3].

Similarly, by 1930, competition between bus operators was intense and in many areas out of control. The three main types of public service vehicle were established, the single decked bus, the double-decked bus and the coach. The charabanc was becoming less common. Save in some areas under adoptive powers or under local acts of parliament there was little or no legal control. There were some notable exceptions. Colonel Howard-Bury (M.P. for Essex and Chelmsford) sought the exclusion of the City of Oxford from the provisions of the proposed general regimen, claiming that under the Oxford and District Tramways Act 1914 and Oxford Motor Services Act 1921 it had already achieved what the new Act was seeking to achieve.[4]

After their appointment the Traffic Commissioners for the Northern Traffic Area found that their area had been 'the cockpit of road transport warfare'. The Western Traffic Area Commissioners noted that there had been 177 local authorities in their area but that only 53 had exercised their powers in relation to public service vehicles and only those to a very limited extent. They lamented:

'In our view if the Road Traffic Act [1930] had operated two years earlier many of the problems which have had to be dealt with would not have arisen, and such as they existed could have been adjusted with relatively little difficulty...

This picture of operations, which led to the need for legislation, seems to have been a common one. The South Eastern Traffic Area Commissioners reported:

'...in the past it would appear that whereas some of these operators have been running to a regular time table a number have not and their services, although at times useful to the public, have not been reliable..

whilst the Northern Scotland Commissioners said:

'...licensing, regulation and control of public service vehicles was not enforced, except in the most important centres of the area, with the result that many road services were unlicensed and operated without time tables and very often cut fares to secure support from the travelling public. Some operators adopted such practices as "chasing", "hanging back", running only at peak hours or

> *only on special occasions, and generally "creaming" the traffic on the road. This intensive form of competition known as "tail racing" was not only unduly wasteful, but constituted a serious menace to the public using the roads.'*[5]

An entertaining picture of these 'bus wars' is to be found in Harry Secombe's book 'Welsh Fargo'[6] chronicling a 'war' between Dai Fargo, running a small operation from his village in a South Wales valley, and the regional transport company in Swansea. This scenario was repeated in the 'bus wars' which followed on from deregulation and privatisation of The National Bus Company and the Scottish Bus Group in the late 1980s.

Whilst municipal bus operations were generally limited to being within the borough many large bus operators had come into existence, sometimes formed by railway companies to complement their train services, sometimes by entrepreneurs. By 1930 it was clear to the Government that a national system of regulation was required, leading to the Road Traffic Act 1930. This introduced a system of what was essentially quantity licensing, which remained substantially unchanged until deregulation under the Transport Act 1985 and its system of quality licensing.

The Act divided England (including Wales) and Scotland into thirteen Traffic Areas,[7] an arrangement which still exists though the number has been reduced by a series of reorganisations to eight with seven Commissioners. The original traffic areas are set out (with slight simplification) in Appendix 1 and the Commissioners from the first are listed in Appendix 2.

The Act created the Traffic Commissioners[8] and provided as follows:

> *'For each traffic area there shall be a body of three commissioners who shall have the power and be charged with the duty of issuing licences under this Part of this Act and shall exercise such powers and perform such other duties as are conferred or imposed on them by or in pursuance of this Act, and subject as aforesaid shall act under the general directions of the Minister.'* [9]

The exception to the rule of three was the Metropolitan Traffic Area where only one Commissioner was appointed,[10] the powers being shared with the Commissioner of the Metropolitan Police.[11] The requirement to act under the general direction of the Minister was something which from time to time they did not all like, but was certainly better than having to act under the directions of the Minister.

During the Committee stage of the Bill[12] (Standing Committee C) Mr Herbert Morrison, the Minister of Transport sought to explain what that meant in terms of the relationship between the Minister and the Commissioners:

'Certainly that relationship is a little subtle, but that is characteristically British, and I am sure that it will work satisfactorily in practice. I am anxious that my power of direction to the Commissioners should not be more than a general power, and I should think it wrong if powers were given to the Minister to give directions in detail rather than on general policy...'

A certain Colonel Ashley (Member for Hants and Christchurch) was not mollified by the answer:

'...they should be under his direction. That is to say, that the Minister will have absolute control over these traffic commissioners, and that there will be no opportunity for any cantankerous traffic commissioner to create troubles between himself and the Minister...'

The Minister was quite clear what he was looking for and it has probably been achieved over the 75 years:

'... in their handling of applications for licences they shall be perfectly free and independent to grant or refuse licences and to attach conditions and do all their duties on their own responsibility, using their own judgment fairly... I want them ... to feel that they are really free, independent men, acting judicially according to the evidence of each case put before them...' [13]

The Chairman, having been appointed by the Minister, was to hold full time office for up to seven years, though was then eligible for re-appointment.[14] Of the other two Commissioners, one was to be appointed from a panel nominated by the county councils and one from a panel nominated by the county boroughs and urban districts in the traffic area.[15] These 'lay' Commissioners only held office for up to three years though were eligible for re-appointment, and frequently were, if their name remained on the panel.[16] Numerous deputies were also appointed. Of course many of the county borough councils operated substantial bus fleets.

Colonel Ashley also urged that no lawyers should be appointed as commissioners:

'I hope the Minister will avoid appointing lawyers for his commissioners. I say it in all seriousness. Lawyers are necessary evils, and we must have them in the body politic, and naturally must look at everything from the legal point of view. But in handling the traffic of this country we want people who will take a broad point of view and perhaps stretch the law a point to get common-sense decisions, and whether there are five, or three, or one commissioner I hope the Minister will keep that point in view...'[17]

During the same meeting the Colonel also had been concerned as to what number of Commissioners there should be, particularly if they were to receive £2000 or £3000 per annum, though he was less concerned if it were to be £500 per annum. Mr. Remer (Member for Chester and Macclesfield) was shocked at the idea they should be paid at all. The Minister was however quite clear that the salary should be one which was adequate to command the type of person that was wanted. He was not then prepared to commit himself to a figure. He was also not averse to the appointment of lawyers:

> *'I should not say that lawyers should be disqualified. I should say that legal knowledge was not necessarily a qualification; the service is one of administration and organisation, and the last thing I should say is that a lawyer is quite incapable of seeing a business proposition. That is not by any means true. I know ... lawyers of very great sense and ability, whom one could trust administratively to do anything...'*

Whilst lawyers may have a slightly uncomfortable feeling that he was damning the profession with faint praise at least three of the first appointments were lawyers including two King's Counsel.[18] After the first appointments a pattern developed, until the 1990s, of the alternate appointment of lawyer, civil servant, member of His or Her Majesty's Armed Forces though the Navy, perhaps understandably, was never represented.

2 First Commissioners appointed

The Traffic Commissioners still exist, though now reduced to one for each area with each having a number of deputies. Then, as now, no particular qualification was required either to be appointed a Commissioner or a deputy, though the Act required that they made a declaration as to what, if any, financial interest they had in any transport undertaking which carried passengers[19] and this was a continuing duty whilst they remained in office.[20] Provided there was no such financial conflict the Minister could only remove a Commissioner for 'inability or misbehaviour'.[21] They seem all to have been able and as far as we know of good behaviour because in 1937 the terms of their appointment were changed so that they held office 'during His Majesty's pleasure'[22] though those appointed after the new Act were to vacate office on attaining the age of seventy.

The Commissioners were appointed with effect from 1 January 1931 with the operational provisions of the Act coming into force on the 1 April 1931 (a popular date for the introduction of much subsequent legislation). They were required to report annually to the Minister and their first report covered the period from 1 January 1931 to 31 March 1932. From the beginning meetings, generally known as Traffic Commissioners' Conferences, were held with full-time civil servants (very occasionally with the Minister present for part) generally twice a year. The somewhat secretive nature of these meetings is revealed in a minute of a meeting which took place on 20 January 1933:

'They agreed...that the decision should be given as the decision of the Commissioners concerned and that no reference should be made as to the decision of the Conference.

The Secretary said that, whereas uniformity of practice was desirable he assumed that the Commissioners in giving their decision on individual ap-

plications never referred to any general decision reached by the Chairmen at one of their meetings...'

The first such 'conference' was held on 21 January 1931 when the Minister took the chair. He informed the Commissioners that the object of the Act was to secure a more efficient and co-ordinated traffic service; that their duties included the administration and organization (sic) of traffic; and, that they would be responsible for their own decisions. The meeting, then under the chairmanship of a certain Sir Cyril Hurcomb, went on to discuss many detailed matters.[23]

A second meeting quickly followed on 27 February 1931. It is not clear who was the author of the note, but he had some bold views about the conduct of the decision making process:

'I strongly pressed that we should give no reason accompanying a decision. A pretty strong discussion took place on this. Strangely enough the lawyers appeared to incline towards giving reasons. However on putting it to the vote there was a very decisive majority for giving no reasons, Mr. Rowland Harker [South Eastern Traffic Area], who was acting as chairman was asked to convey that decision to Sir Cyril...'

What Sir Cyril thought of that suggestion we do not know. Later, on 11 July 1931 Sir Cyril asked the Commissioners about their practice. Mr. W. Chamberlain, [North-Western Traffic Area], Mr. Archibald Henderson, [Southern Scotland Traffic Area] and Mr. Joseph Farndale, [Yorkshire Traffic Area] all said that it was not their practice to give reasons, with Mr. Henderson adding that in his opinion giving reasons would merely be a source of argument, and would be more likely to lead to an appeal to the Minister than if no reasons were given. Perhaps there is a faint 'Hear, hear!' from Commissioners who down the years have seen their decisions dissected and analysed by successive Ministers and the Transport Tribunal. Mr Henry Riches, [Northern Traffic Area] and Mr. Rowand Harker, [South-Eastern Traffic Area] said they always gave reasons, whilst Mr. A. F. Nicholson, [Western Traffic Area] and Mr. Gleeson E. Robinson, [Metropolitan Traffic Area] gave their main reasons.

Sir E. Haviland Hiley, [Eastern Traffic Area], Mr. A. T. James, [South Wales Traffic Area] and Colonel A. S. Redman, [West Midland Traffic Area] gave reasons in cases where the application was for new services.

Sir John Maxwell, [Northern Scotland Traffic Area] and Major-General Sir Reginald Ford, [Southern Traffic Area] had each only been asked twice and only Sir John had given reasons and that on one occasion. Mr. J. H. Stirk, [East Midland Traffic Area] took a philosophical approach saying that he occasionally gave reasons, but he did not think the giving or failing to give reasons had any effect on the number of appeals that were made, since he was convinced that in most cases appeals were made to enable the applicant to continue to run a service.

Perhaps of equal importance to the Commissioners at that conference was the inadequacy of allowances for expenses (especially of the lay Commissioners) particularly when sitting at seaside resorts at the height of the season. This appears to be the first of many occasions over the years upon which the Commissioners raised the issue of allowances. Sir Cyril gave them what became almost a standard reply; that he had gone into the matter with the Treasury, but that there were serious difficulties in the way of altering a recognised scale of allowances. Some small increase was eventually allowed but it did not satisfy the Commissioners and on 12 August 1933 Sir Cyril Hurcomb wrote to them again via the Chairman of their then most recent Conference, Mr. E. Haviland Hiley:

> *'I am to point out that the scales of travelling and other allowances of Traffic Commissioners have been under consideration on more than one occasion and authority was obtained for a special rate of allowance in 1932. Whilst the grounds for the Chairmen's perturbation are appreciated, it is feared that there is no prospect of the Ministry being able to obtain any further concession in this matter in present circumstances...'*

The issue of the conduct of proceedings and of giving reasons had not gone away. During a meeting which extended from 7 to 9 January 1932 Sir Cyril was reported as saying, in the best civil service 'speak':

> *'... [he] had no desire to level any general criticism at the form or scope of the Commissioners' observations on appeals. There had however, been isolated cases in which the facts had not been stated accurately or in full correspondence with the recorded evidence, other cases in which the reasons given had been inadequate or even irrelevant, and yet other cases in which the language adopted had perhaps been a little unguarded or, on the other hand, not quite dispassionate, for example, in one recent case which had come under his notice an observation began: "There is not an atom of truth in the appellant's statement, etc". Language of this kind reflected heat rather than light on the matter at issue.*
>
> *Though cases of the kind to which he referred had been few, they had notwithstanding proved very embarrassing. The Commissioners had perhaps not at this outset realised in all cases the immense importance attached to every word of their observations by the appellants and counsel...*
>
> *The Minister wished the prestige of the Commissioners to be maintained and increased as far as possible, and he, the Secretary, thought that any*

means, however small, for increasing this prestige should be adopted. As an illustration he mentioned that he had been informed that in one area the Chairman of the Traffic Commissioners sat at a public sitting with his two colleagues sitting on one hand and members of his office staff on the other. He suggested that perhaps the dignity of the Traffic Commissioners would be upheld better if the Chairman sat with one colleague on either hand...'

But he did not leave it there:

'...[he] said that it was a matter of considerable importance that an applicant for a licence, particularly if an application was going to be refused, should have before he left the public sitting, some indication of the view the Commissioners took of his application. The Commissioners by giving reasons for their decisions would, no doubt, go a long way to avoid any charge of arbitrary conduct. He thought, moreover, though this perhaps was open to question, that by giving reasons for their decisions, the Commissioners would discourage applicants from appealing to the Minister... He impressed upon the Chairmen that they should take great care at the time of the public sitting to record the grounds on which they had reached their decision...'

Sir Cyril established that Sir John Maxwell, Mr. Stirk and Colonel Redman had changed their practice and gave reasons and were encouraged by the fact that applicants appeared to be more satisfied and lodged fewer appeals. Sir Cyril emphasised that he was not pressing the Chairmen to alter their practice. He would enquire again at the next meeting. Effectively that was the end of unreasoned decisions, but not of his concerns as to the ways the Traffic Commissioners were carrying out their duties. He continued to hand out mild 'rockets' which no doubt struck home with the Commissioners concerned. At the April 1932 meeting:

'No doubt it was the especial duty of the Chairmen to see that their decisions were, so far as possible, consistent with one another, but the criticism had been made that in certain areas, on points which had often been considered, decisions are occasionally given which strike off in an apparently new direction, without the parties having any reason to believe that the Commissioners were going to take such a line...'

Equal opportunities in this period before the Second World War were not uppermost in their minds. At the same meeting it was noted that they had discretion:

'...to attach conditions to road service licences to the effect, for instance, that no women conductors were to be used on the service...'

There is no doubt that the burden those first Commissioners faced was immense. They had little precedent to follow and, save for the lawyers amongst them, probably little experience of public hearings though some had been JPs. Whilst there are no exact figures available for the number of operators before 1 April 1931, by 31 March 1932 they had licensed 6434 operators between them operating 46,230 public service vehicles. A picture of the industry as it then was is given by the facts that 2760 operators only had one vehicle and 1336 had only two vehicles.[24] The exercise was one that had to start from scratch though to some extent with one arm tied behind their backs. The Minister had made it clear that:

> '...*it would be an impossible state of affairs for the commissioners to appoint their own staff as to numbers, qualifications and salaries*...' [25]

Mr. Henry Riches recorded in his first annual report:

> '*The Chairman and Clerk to the Commissioners, together with a skeleton staff assumed duty on 1 January 1931, and devoted most of their time during the first 2 months to building up the office organisation, selecting the necessary indoor and outdoor staff, and advising operators generally as to the steps they should take to carry out the new statutory obligations laid upon them*...'

One wonders how they would have coped had they had to wait for a computer system?

3 Powers and control

The Commissioners had huge powers from the beginning but were to exercise their powers in public. They were under an obligation, when hearing and determining applications for the grant of licences, to sit in public and might also do so for '...any other purpose, if they so think fit...'[26]

They were given control of who might operate bus and coach services by the requirement that such persons be the holders of public service vehicle licences[27] and it was through this provision that they were able to exercise a level of control over the condition of vehicles.[28] They were given the control of the operation of public service vehicles used for stage carriage or express carriage in their traffic area through 'road service licences'[29] with power to grant 'backings' for services commencing outside their area. Stage carriages were what we would today recognise as local bus services. The Commissioners were prohibited from granting a licence if they considered speed limits would be contravened on the route and had to have regard to:

- suitability of the route
- the extent to which the route or part of it was already adequately served
- the extent to which the proposed service was necessary or desirable in the public interest
- the needs of the area as a whole...and the co-ordination of all forms of passenger transport, including transport by rail.[30]

They were also given power to attach conditions and in particular for securing that:

- the fares were not unreasonable (in fact for 55 years they fixed the fares using the specific power to do so first set out in section 72(6))
- timetables and fare tables were available

- passengers were only to be picked up and set down at specified places,
- and generally for securing the safety and convenience of the public.[31]

Commissioners could only grant road service licences for lengths of road in their own traffic areas. As soon as a route departed from one traffic area to another a 'backing' was required[32] when the commissioners for that traffic area could impose their own conditions.[33]

Perhaps still concerned about unfair trading or competition, a requirement was placed on applicants for or the holders of licences to provide Commissioners with details of any agreements or arrangements with other providers of passenger transport facilities in the area, any financial interest which any other passenger transport provider had in the holders business, or he had in another's business.[34]

Thus we see the beginnings of the control of buses and coaches removed from a free for all era of competition to the control of the Traffic Commissioners which they substantially retained until the Transport Act 1985. Hand in hand with the power to grant public service vehicle licences and road service licences, commenced the disciplinary powers of the Commissioners. They might revoke or suspend a public service vehicle licence having regard to the conduct of the holder of the licence or the manner in which a vehicle was used, if it appeared that such person was not a fit person to hold such a licence.[35]

The Commissioners were also empowered to revoke or suspend a road service licence if any condition subject to which it been granted had not been complied with,[36] provided they were satisfied that it was appropriate owing to the frequency of breach, the wilfulness of the breach or the danger to the public involved in the breach.

But this was not the limit of the powers given to the Commissioners nor the systems and procedures they had to put in place from 1 April 1931. Also within their remit fell certificates of fitness for public service vehicles[37] and drivers' and conductors' licensing.[38] Perhaps it now seems surprising that that they were also to be concerned with the terms and conditions of employment of those employed 'in connection with the operation of a public service vehicle.' Any organisation representing such employees could complain to the Commissioners who could, through the Minister, refer the matter to the Industrial Court.[39] In due course the same provisions were extended to the road haulage industry.[40]

It is difficult now to appreciate the burden with which these first Commissioners coped. Some picture can be gained from the workload. In the period up to 31 March 1932 the Northern Commissioners received 1818 applications for road service licences, and 624 applications for backings. They sat on 146 days in 25 different locations to deal with those applications to which there were 3500 objections. Whilst doing that they dealt with applications from 5303 drivers (of whom three were women) and of course with the applications for public service vehicle licences and certificates of fitness. They commented that the task they faced was of:

> *'...considerable magnitude, intensified by the urgent need for national economy, which made it necessary to carry out the new duties with the minimum staff...'*[41]

There were not dissimilar workloads in other traffic areas. The Yorkshire Commissioners sat on 107 days; the North Western on 131 having received 4450 applications. The East Midland received 4231 applications and the Eastern 5318 sitting on 94 days to dispose of them. The South Wales Traffic Area received 2330 applications for licences and backings, sitting on 72 days at 15 locations. The Western Commissioners received a similar number of applications for licences and backings and 2117 objections, 753 from operators, 764 from local authorities and 600 from railway companies. In the South East the Commissioners sat on 161 days, the chairman on each occasion, to deal with 2084 applications for licences and 1796 for backings. The combined total for Scotland was 5207 applications for licences and backings with 95 sittings.

The Commissioners were not particularly helped by the applicants. The current Commissioners might say that there is nothing new in that.

> *'...certain operators were obviously ploughing a lonely furrow and were the cause of much perturbation to the members of our staff who in certain cases had to interview such operators when repeated attempts to put their applications in order by means of correspondence had failed...' (Yorkshire T.A.)*
>
> *'...a flood of applications received all at the same time as most applicants for licences delayed sending in their applications until the last moment, with the result that at the end of March the staff were inundated with applications which could not possibly have been dealt with without great delay if necessary arrangements had not been made in anticipation...'*[42]

The picture was a common one. The Yorkshire Commissioners reported that on commencement the indoor and outdoor (e.g. vehicle examiners) staff, in addition to the Commissioner and the Clerk, totalled 11 and by the end of the year had only increased to 18. With true Yorkshire grit the Commissioners had determined:

'We decided that we should complete all cases in the list for hearing on each day. This decision was meant to obviate operators being put to un-necessary expense and inconvenience by having their cases deferred from day to day. We feel sure that operators have appreciated our action. In consequence late sittings were by no means uncommon and in our first year we sat on one night as late as 10.45 but even this hour has been surpassed in the current year...'[43]

The South Scotland Commissioners adopted a similar policy, though what the lawyers thought of it is not recorded or was perhaps not recordable. One of the advantages of shorthand writers taking the transcript rather than the tape recording of inquiries was that they could occasionally be deaf:

'...it was necessary on many occasions for the Commissioners to sit for long hours on successive days to enable all the cases in the list to be disposed of...'

'...At the public sittings occupied in hearing the initial applications for licences most of the operators employed legal assistance...'[44]

And so the system got under way though with 1309 appeals to the Minister under section 81 of which at 31 March 1932, 635 were still outstanding (322 against the grant of a licence, 440 by operators in relation to conditions attached to their licences and one in relation to the suspension of a PSV licence). These figures no doubt gave rise to the concern that Sir Cyril Hurcomb had been expressing at the Traffic Commissioners' meetings.

Mr. A. F. Nicholson said of himself and his fellow commissioners, and which could probably be said to have applied to date:

'We have done our best to arrive at decisions which were fair, impartial and in accordance with the evidence presented to us, ... it would be surprising if we had not made some errors of judgement...'[45]

He also noted that lawyers had made a strong appearance on the scene:

'In almost the whole of the cases where objections had been laid by the railway companies the parties concerned were legally represented...'

Whilst public service vehicle examiners had been part of the system from the beginning, it had become apparent by the Conference on 21 October 1932 that many breaches of conditions attached to licences were occurring:

'The Chairmen pressed therefore, for the appointment of suitable officers... who would be able to travel about the area and should therefore be equipped with motor cycles, and who could collect evidence and represent the Commissioners in court. These men should be trained in observing and collecting evidence...'

Whilst this came about in due course, it will be no surprise to current Commissioners that Sir Cyril's response was:

> *'...he agreed that the Commissioners must be placed in a position to show quite clearly that when they attached conditions to licences they were going to take steps to see that these conditions were observed. He promised ... to see what steps could be taken to meet the Commissioners' demands, although in view of the difficulty at the moment of adding further officers to the Commissioners' establishments ... it would be a great advantage if the Commissioners could find in their present staff, officers capable of doing it...'*

4 Salter and goods vehicle licensing

By the time of the Commissioner's meeting on 20 January 1933, Sir Cyril was able to report that officers might be appointed by the Commissioners to be called "Public Service Vehicle (Traffic) Examiners."

This was the time of the "Salter" Report considering the licensing of goods vehicles. The Traffic Commissioners clearly saw a role for themselves. Indeed over the years the Commissioners have tended to go from glut to famine as far as their volume of work was concerned. It is even rumoured that one Commissioner of the North Western Traffic Area suggested in the 1980s, to the horror of his colleagues, that their posts should be made part-time. Mr. A. T. James, appointed chairman for the particular meeting, is recorded in the following way:

> *'He pointed out that the "Salter" Report does not suggest to what licensing authority the duties of licensing goods vehicles should be given. It would be easier to give it to the Traffic Commissioners if it could be shown first that they have so far organised the licensing of public service vehicles that they would have time to devote to this new work, and secondly that the procedure which they have adopted in licensing public service vehicles is not over elaborate...'*

The reaction of his colleagues was not recorded. He was to get his way.

The quantity licensing of goods vehicles has a long history. The Common Council of the City of London in 1681 limited the number of carts or 'carrs' to 420 and required that each should be licensed and marked, a custom which is still remembered by The Worshipful Company of Carmen who each year hold a ceremony of cart marking at the Guildhall.

The Report led to the Road and Rail Traffic Act 1933 which received the Royal Assent on 17 November 1933. Section 1(1) provided quite simply:

'Subject to the provisions of this Part of this Act, no person shall use a goods vehicle on a road for the carriage of goods –

(a) for hire or reward; or
(b) for or in connection with any trade or business carried on by him, except under a licence.'

Licences were subdivided into:
(i) public carriers' licences ('A' licences)
(ii) limited carriers' licences ('B' licences)
(iii) private carriers licences ('C' licences)

This system remained substantially unchanged, save for the war years and a short period of nationalisation, until it was finally phased out in 1971 under the Transport Act 1968.

The Traffic Commissioners secured their interest under section 4(1):

'The person who is the chairman of the traffic commissioners for any traffic area ... shall have the power and be charged with the duty of granting licences...and is in this Part of the Act referred to as "the licensing authority".'

Section 4(2) made the necessary adjustment for the fact that there was a sole commissioner in the Metropolitan Traffic Area.

Section 7 gave protection to those who had been in the haulage business with motor vehicles prior to 1 April 1932. Provided they applied before the 1 April 1934 they were entitled to licences for an equivalent aggregate value of the unladen weight they had been operating. Private carriers licences were not so limited. The entitlement was an 'A' licence if the previous operation had been solely for hire or reward, or a 'B' licence if the vehicles had been used in part for hire or reward and partly for other purposes.

Whilst the Act was primarily concerned with quantity licensing it was a standard condition of every licence under section 8:

'...that the authorised vehicles are maintained in a fit and serviceable condition;'

Section 12 gave the licensing authority power, after holding a public enquiry if the holder of the licence so requested, to revoke or suspend a licence on the ground that any condition of the licence had not been complied with.

The Minister had perhaps learned his lesson that the Commissioners were capable of causing a very large number of appeals to be generated and was not prepared to risk it a second time. This time he decided that appeals should be to an Appeal Tribunal. There was already in existence the Canal and Rail Traffic Appeal Tribunal which in 1935 became the Road and Rail Traffic Appeal Tribunal under the Road and Rail Traffic Appeal Tribunal Rules 1934. In due course this became the Transport Tribunal and is still hearing many appeals from the Commissioners. It was soon under way hearing its first appeal on 11 September 1934 (Edwards' Appeal – A9) when it held, not unsurprisingly, that an operator could not appeal against a condition to which he had agreed.

The Act also provided for the keeping of records of hours worked, journeys, loads etc. Section 17 provided for the enforcement of the obligation to maintain goods vehicles and for the appointment of "examiners" for that purpose with powers, inter alia, to prohibit vehicles. Licensing of heavy goods vehicle drivers was not introduced until section 31 Road Traffic Act 1934 and of course that became the responsibility of the chairman of the traffic commissioners wearing his hat as licensing authority.

The Act also abolished the Southern Traffic Area and re-organised the East Midland and Eastern Traffic Areas. Sir Rowand Harker the original South Eastern Commissioner became Chairman of the Road and Rail Tribunal and Sir Henry Piggott became Chairman of the newly enlarged South Eastern Traffic Area.

By their Conference on 20 October 1933 the Commissioners had come under pressure to agree to bring the Act into operation on 1 July 1934. Sir Cyril was already concerned about any increase in the Traffic Area staff:

> *'In regard to temporary staff recruited locally he said that a memorandum would be issued but asked the Chairmen to bear in mind that the services of such temporary staff would have to be dispensed with as soon as possible as such employment could not be made a means of permanent entry into the service...'*

At the Conference on 20 April 1934 the Chairmen were already backtracking on the commencement date for 'A' and 'B' licences opining that 1 October was the earliest date. Again the Commissioners would be faced with carrying out a huge volume of work in a short period of time.

The Appeal Tribunal quickly became active and the road haulage industry and its customers had to adapt to a new commercial world controlled by the Licensing Authorities:

> *'Since Parliament has granted to licensing authorities a discretion to grant or refuse licences, traders no longer have the right to choose the carriers they will employ...'*[46]
>
> *'A trader who carries his own goods long distances to deliver to his customers, and on the return journey carries goods for his customers for reward, competes with carriers who only carry for reward, and it is not desirable in the interests of transport that he should so...'*[47]

5 Public sittings and reports

In the midst of all this change the Commissioners continued with their duties under the 1930 Act, though they seemed to be getting the hang of giving reasoned and supportable decisions because the 1934/5 Annual Report indicated that they had got the number of appeals down to 712 in the relevant 12 months.

The number of public sittings for all purposes connected with road service and public service vehicle licensing had reduced across all traffic areas, though it must be remembered that Traffic Commissioners have always had considerable discretion when it came to the exercise of their powers.

The Northern Traffic Area reported only 60 days of sittings with no adjournments. Like other Areas they were becoming concerned as to how unremunerative services should be dealt with; a problem which was to remain with them until deregulation.

> *'...the co-ordination of services and the absorption of small operators has given rise in certain circumstances to claimed inadequacy of the curtailed services provided. These complaints are not confined to any particular locality, there would appear to be a tendency for operators to reduce their mileage too drastically...'*

They were of the opinion;

> *'... that mileage should be eliminated only by a gradual process and then not until it has been ascertained by experience and careful study of the needs of the area served, to what extent the service can be reduced without inconvenience to the travelling public, whose needs must be the first consideration. It is within the knowledge of the Commissioners that a lower frequency of service does not necessarily have the effect of improving the revenue particularly if the service is reduced from a regular frequency to the operations of journeys at irregular intervals. Nor does an increase in fares necessarily increase revenue.*

The law of diminishing return is universal in its application and a road transport operator is not exempt from its effects...'

Similar statements were to be echoed time and time again in the 1960s and 1970s.

Many of the applications made to the Commissioners may have seemed minor but they were considered in detail by them. Applications to bring back people from the military tattoo at Ravensworth Castle, for example, received short shrift

'...the operators were informed the Commissioners' view their obligation to provide transport after the tattoo did not include the provision of special services for belated revellers, and that any member of the public who found themselves thus stranded would doubtless derive considerable benefit from walking home. They were informed that any complaints that were made on that score should be made to the Commissioners. None were received.'

The Yorkshire Commissioners were a little disappointed by the continuing volume of road service licensing disputes

'We had expected, that with the various co-ordination schemes in full working order, that objections would have diminished in number, but this expectation has not been realised. Applications for new licences and services with modifications continue to be received in considerable numbers and these draw as much opposition as ever...'

Commissioners from their earliest reports indicated an interest in the development of transport in their areas. The West Midland Commissioners noted an interesting bus development that eventually became a common design feature:

'...Birmingham and Midland Motor Omnibus Company Limited, which operates throughout most of the area, has on the other hand an experimental single deck vehicle of interesting design. The 40hp engine is mounted transversely at the rear under the back row of seats so that the whole length of the chassis is available for seating passengers. As a result it is possible to arrange seats for 41 passengers in this type of vehicle. The entrance is at the extreme front alongside the driver...'

The same Commissioners tried to disabuse the industry of what they saw as a heresy, though it had a long and possibly continuing life:

'Some misapprehension appears still to exist as to the functions of the Traffic Commissioners. The commissioners are not dictators...'

Whilst the Chairmen had been advised that conditions could be placed on licences against the employment of women as conductors, they had made little progress on the driving front. The South Wales Commissioners noted that only one woman was licensed as a PSV driver.

Perhaps the same commissioners sometimes had the wool pulled over their eyes, if that is, their heads were not buried in the sand. In relation to amalgamations and absorptions they recorded:

> *'...We also should like to state in clear and definite terms that in no case in our experience has a small operator been forced out by competition from the larger operators but that in all cases the small operator, when he has parted from his business has secured terms which have been advantageous to him, which he has generally been pleased to accept...At the same time we must say that we cannot help regarding the passing of the small owner driver operator with considerable misgivings. There can be no doubt that many of the small local services owe their inception to the pioneering spirit of the local man and their success very largely to his personal influence and interest, and we are not without anxiety as to how far the larger operators, deprived of that personal touch which was so characteristic of the smaller operator, will be able to serve the public in the faithful way in which their predecessor did...'*

The South Eastern Traffic Area Commissioners gave themselves a pat on the back, noting that the standard of maintenance of PSVs [i.e. public service vehicles] was considerably higher than when the Act had come into force four years previously.

The same Commissioners had also started imposing conditions on the licences of all operators to the Bettshanger Colliery

> *'...that no vehicle which has been used at any time to carry coal in the previous 14 days shall be used on a passenger service to and from the pit...'*

Any current operator who has received a PG9 for dusty seats must feel slightly hard done by.

North Scotland Traffic Area highlights the extent to which coach excursions were popular in those pre-war traffic free days. They found it necessary to impose conditions on popular excursions – there were to be six groups of vehicles in convoys of six vehicles each, with 300 yards between each vehicle in the convoy and one mile between each convoy.

Mobile phones distracting drivers were obviously something for the future, but the Commissioners at their Conference on 3 May 1935 had not dissimilar concerns:

> *'The Conference decided to make recommendations to the Minister to the effect that he should prohibit by Regulation broadcasting by wireless sets on public service vehicles at any rate whilst the vehicle is in motion, as the conference felt that such a practice is liable to distract the driver's attention with consequent danger to the public...'*

Perhaps, however, Sir Cyril had a wireless set in his car:

> *'Sir Cyril Hurcomb stated that there was no evidence in the possession of the Ministry to indicate that this practice involved danger, at any rate in private cars...'*

Travelling expenses were raised again in the hope of entitling public service vehicle examiners authorised to use a motorcar to have a motorcar allowance and, where necessary traffic examiners should be allowed to use a motor vehicle.

> *'Sir Cyril Hurcomb pointed out that Parliament was apt to be very critical of travelling expenses, but stated that the Ministry would give favourable consideration to applications for the grant of the minimum allowance for a car to traffic examiners where the Chairman was able to recommend that it was to the advantage of the work that a car should be used...'*

[I make a personal digression here to note that my predecessor and mentor Thomas Denner Corpe (see footnote p104) made his first appearance in the Court of the Transport Tribunal on 15 May 1935 on an appeal for his clients Hawker Ltd against the Great Western Railway Company and the London and Midland and Scottish Railway Company.[48] It was a good start, the Tribunal commenting on his grasp of Euston & Co and London Midland and Scottish Railway Company [cases]:[49]

> *'It is clear that there has been and is no confusion in Mr Corpe's mind on the subject and he fully appreciated the effect of that decision...That part of Mr Corpe's argument which we have quoted so closely coincides with our own views that it is unnecessary for us to say anything more than that we agree with it...']*

The Traffic Commissioners continued to pursue the issue of travel allowances for their staff making a further recommendation at their Conference on 18 October 1935:

> *'The conference agreed that the Ministry should be asked to agree to the compound rate of 2¼d. per mile appropriate for cars of up to 8hp granted to those Senior Vehicle Examiners who necessarily use cars in the course of their duties...'*

6 Heavy workloads

By the time of the Conference on 16 and 17 January 1936 the Chairmen were perhaps beginning to doubt the wisdom of having sought to add carriers' licensing to their duties. They recommended that the duration of 'B' licences should be extended to two years. Sir Cyril was not impressed:

> *'After he had been informed that the basis of the proposal was a reduction in the burden of work now falling on the licensing authorities Sir Cyril Hurcomb said there might be serious objection to such a proposal on the grounds of general policy...'*

It may be thought that the use of motorcycles (or mopeds) for the carriage of goods (pizzas and other take-aways) is a new phenomenon but the Chairmen were tackling this problem at their Conference on 16 October 1936:

> *'The Conference recorded that, if motor cycles are constructed or adapted for the carriage of goods, carriers' licences are necessary... it was agreed that it would be undesirable to start anything in the nature of a campaign to enforce their being licensed...'*

They had enough work to do already!

The Commissioners were becoming far more interested in the general development of the road passenger industry as they became more knowledgeable and received more feed back from the public and operators. Over the years they showed an interest in the defects in and the development of buses and coaches. In the 1935/6 Report the Commissioner for the Northern Traffic Area noted:

> *'The ventilation of many vehicles is still inadequate and some new vehicles have been examined in which no special arrangement for ventilation has in fact been provided. This problem has been rendered more acute by the increasing use of heaters. A future development might possibly lie in the direction of some system of air conditioning for public service vehicles...'*

Whilst his colleague in the Yorkshire Traffic Area was taking a much more positive view of vehicles in his area:

> *'Some stage carriages are now almost as fully equipped as the luxury touring coaches with mirrors, luggage racks, ash trays and warm air ventilation with thermostatic control...'*

Though he could not resist recommending the:

> *'...desirability of the daily disinfection of public service vehicles...'*

The East Midland Commissioner was quite carried away by the visual beauty and engineering sophistication of the new types of vehicle:

> *'The effect of these flowing lines and streamlining within the limits of seating capacity and permissible dimensions show marked ingenuity and a keen sense of beauty of outline on the part of the body builders... many vehicles have hand brakes and foot brakes operating on all four wheels...'*

From time to time the Commissioners were made aware of the social consequences of their decisions. Over a number of years there was discussion as to whether a ticket issued as a return ticket could be used twice in the same direction instead of as a 'there and back again' ticket. It seems likely that they had not considered all the implications until the North Commissioner received a letter:

> *'The position was viewed from a novel stand-point by a public-spirited but anonymous citizen who averred that the request to be allowed to use return tickets either way must be seriously considered by the Commissioners owing to the repercussions refusal would have on local social conditions. These tickets, according to the correspondence, are extensively used by "lads from pit villages who take a bus to some other village on a return ticket, walk back with their lasses and then leave them to return home on the return half." He gloomily prophesied that the effect of the Commissioners' refusal to sanction such use would reduce courting in the colliery districts by quite 25 per cent...'*

Though perhaps the "lads" would have been pleased to note, as did the Commissioner for the North-Western Traffic Area:

> *'The tendency for stage carriage fares generally to be reduced has continued...'*

The West Midland Commissioner thanked his Clerk Mr S W Nelson for his services and congratulated him on his appointment as Chairman of the Central Transport Licensing Board of the Federated Malay States. In 1949 Mr S W Nelson was Chairman of the Traffic Commissioners for the Northern Traffic Area before moving to the Western Traffic Area.

The Northern Scotland Commissioner was concerned with a much more serious matter, the weather, though even he could wax a little lyrical:

> *'It is impossible to do more than touch on the innumerable adventures, grave and gay, which befell drivers, conductors and their passengers... During a blizzard a car ran into a snowdrift near Dundee and an omnibus and a dozen other vehicles became wedged behind it on the snow and ice; the passengers... and the other travellers were fortunate in being able to reach a nearby village where they sheltered... A frequent difficulty was that, in the fury of wind, telegraph poles were blown down, and lay in a maze of wires across the road. It became almost a matter of routine to dig a vehicle out of the snow...'*

The Southern Scotland Traffic Area seems to have missed this severe weather because the Commissioner found the following most noteworthy:

> *'The sailing of the "Queen Mary" from the Clyde on 24 March 1936 was the occasion for many applications for special services and facilities...'*

The Northern Scotland Commissioner found the next winter even more exciting:

> *'The winter of 1936/7 was the most severe in this area within living memory...From the 29 January, considerable lengths of the road service routes... became blocked with snow and rendered impassable...before normal conditions had returned, hard frosts and heavy intermittent showers of rain and sleet caused the roads to become ice bound and by the middle of February it seemed that vehicular traffic would be brought to a standstill...towards the end of February, the northern parts of Scotland, which had also shared the heavy weather experienced elsewhere...now suffered the worst snow storm since 1881. Roads became impassable and a large number of vehicles became snow bound ... many of the principal routes were cleared by the early days of March, but in the outlying districts, especially in the hilly regions, the enormous amounts of snow and ice were slow to disappear...The Commissioners have pleasure in paying a tribute of praise and appreciation to the meritorious service and courageous spirit of the drivers and the conductors...'*

The impact of adverse weather conditions was initially relatively minor in the Northern Traffic Area:

> *'The sliding roof appears to be declining in popularity, possibly on account of general climatic conditions...'*

However he was able to come into contention with his Northern Scotland colleague in December 1937:

> *'During the greater part of December, operators generally were faced with exceptional difficulties...on account of the unusually severe climatic conditions.*

Heavy snow-storms intermittently swept the country, growing in intensity until many roads became extremely dangerous and difficult to negotiate owing to the icy surfaces; some routes became impassable owing to snow-drifts... Considerable expense was incurred by the operators in the provision of clearance gangs and the transport of sand for use on the roads...Only when it was considered too great a risk to life and limb or when conditions became impossible was any service completely suspended, and the Commissioners are pleased to pay tribute to the operators and their staffs...'

7 Clouds of war

By this time the clouds of war must have been seen to be gathering on the horizon, but nothing in their Conferences in April or July 1937 suggested this. They were still discussing whether the duration of 'B' licences should be two years or some different period when regulations were made under the Road Traffic Act 1937.

1936/1937 was the year of the Third Annual Report of the Commissioners wearing their hats as Licensing Authorities. The system of carriers' licensing had in general begun to settle down though the workload remained heavy. The Licensing Authority for the Northern Traffic Area reported that 76 public sittings had been held and that during the twelve months 1584 applications (20.8 per sitting) attracting 1836 objections had been dealt with. The Railways accounted for 68.6 per cent of the objections. He lamented however:

> *'Notwithstanding the lapse of time since the inception of the Act, many operators...continue to find difficulty in understanding and complying with its requirements. During the last year no fewer than 6557 persons visited my office seeking guidance and assistance in regard to the completion of their applications, their statutory obligations, and so on...'*

The examination of the condition of goods vehicles was clearly established as part of the regime of the Licensing Authorities and as in all subsequent Annual Reports they gave details. The same traffic area examined 6485 vehicles of which they found 2135 to be defective, in some cases quite alarmingly so:

> *'...several cases have been noted where the rear overhang...has caused little or no weight to be placed on the front wheels. When such vehicles are being driven at ordinary speeds there is a tendency for the front wheels to bounce along the roads and thus render the vehicle incapable of being properly*

controlled. In fact, in one instance a vehicle examiner was able to raise the front wheels of a vehicle entirely clear of the ground by raising the front bumper...'

It must not be forgotten that the horse was still the motive power for much goods transport and of course not subject to the 1933 Act. The Licensing authorities had to tackle that problem:

'The railway companies...have also continued steadily their policy of horse substitution – indeed the Railway formula of "a motor vehicle for a horse and a half" is widely quoted from end to end of the Area by road hauliers, in support of their applications for replacement of horses by motor vehicles...'

The Yorkshire Traffic Area continued to be one of the busiest holding 190 days of public sittings for goods vehicle issues. These concentrated very much on the battle between the railways and road transport. The Licensing Authority summarised the objections made by the railway companies as being:

'(i) In so far as the objectors provide commercially suitable transport facilities, a grant of further facilities would involve an excess over requirements.

(ii) An excess of suitable transport facilities over requirements meant wasteful competition.

(iii) Wasteful competition was not in the public interest.

(iv) A grant which caused wasteful competition was not in the public interest...'

though he did not seem to be overly impressed by that argument.

The North-Western Traffic Area gave an interesting picture of the road haulage industry as it then existed. Fifty per cent of 'A' licence holders had only one vehicle and the average was only 2.8 vehicles per operator. Perhaps this preponderance of one-vehicle operators, probably using vehicles that had seen service in 1914-1918, accounts for the overall poor standard of vehicles in use:

'It is worthy of note...that approximately one in every seven of the vehicles subject to prohibition notices was in such a state that apparently the owner did not consider it worth while to endeavour to effect repairs...'

Rogues seem always to have existed in the road haulage industry and one can sometimes almost sense that Licensing Authorities had a certain degree of tolerance for them. There was an understatement from the Licensing Authority for the East Midlands Traffic Area:

'I did have some difficulty with an applicant for the renewal of his licence whose vehicle had been prohibited, whose drivers' records were lost, who did

not know the name of his chief customer and whose knowledge of receipts seemed limited to the pocket money his wife allowed him...'

The same Licensing Authority also received interesting reports from his vehicle examiners:

'A trailer containing three lions was found to have no brakes, although pseudo brake connections were shown between the tractor and the trailer...'

'During checks on the road it is not uncommon to see several drivers adjusting brakes, tightening loose bolts and carrying our repairs...'

'The use of trailers drawn by private cars to avoid the licensing of a goods vehicle and the keeping of records is on the increase. It is a quite common sight in this Area to see a private car full of market garden produce drawing a trailer also loaded. Sometimes the trailers carry as many as 20 sheep or even two beasts...'

'...owing to the rapidity with which news spreads that a check is being carried out, results may be disappointing after four hours. During the check at Stamford on 22 February, 1937, by about 4am. a lorry driver stated that the check was known in London...'

Speed cameras and other automatic electronic surveillance equipment had not been invented but lorry drivers were years ahead of the times in contemplating it. A major check was carried out in Lincolnshire:

'A noticeable feature of the check was the poor illumination or dirty condition of many of the identification plates of goods vehicles. It would seem impossible to come to any other conclusion than that the plates were in a large number of cases being deliberately disfigured or partly obliterated in order to make identification difficult...'

The Licensing Authority for the Eastern Traffic Area did seem to be aware of the changing international scene:

'A feature of the year has been applications received, especially from the LNER, for authorisation of vehicles for conveying material to be used in the construction of aerodromes in the East of England...'

though with an interesting variation of 'the war will be over by Christmas' he only granted licences for nine months,

The Licensing Authority for the North Scotland Traffic Area was proud to record that during the year he had travelled 6400 miles by rail and 650 by sea to hold Public Sittings and spent 21 days of those discussing the transportation of fish. The Scottish character showed through into road haulage operations:

'I was much impressed by the evidence given in support of one such application [to carry livestock] by a Perthshire farmer whom I might describe as a typical "canny Scot". He explained that in his neighbourhood farmers nowadays were strongly influenced in the marketing of their stock by the wireless reports of stock prices, and their consignments to the most advantageous market were frequently of the "last minute" type, for which only motor transport was suitable...'

Not for the first time was a Licensing Authority the subject of criticism by an operator for alleged delay in dealing with an application:

'There was...no foundation for the complaint (after submission of a delayed application) by a poetic Hebridean that, owing to my "department's languid decision such transaction between myself and his client had been obliterated..."'

Whereas one might have thought that the horse was more likely to be the surviving motive power in the Northern Scotland Traffic Area it was his colleague in the South Scotland Traffic Area who commented on that aspect of haulage:

'I would say that the days of horse-drawn transport are far from finished in this Area and many horse-drawn vehicles are still with us in both country and town...'

His traffic area had also come up with a 'cunning plan' to catch drivers:

'In some cases, two checks in different parts of the same district were carried out concurrently. Drivers could not, therefore be sure, that by a deviation of route they would escape a check of which they had received warning...'

The Annual Report of the Traffic Commissioners for 1937/8 was the last before War. The new Commissioner for the West Midland Traffic Area recorded the retirement of his predecessor, Colonel A. S. Redman. He was the first of the original Commissioners to retire. His successor, Mr H. Trevor Morgan recorded:

'To him fell the difficult task of building up in this Area an organisation to deal with the administration of the Act and also of enforcing the provisions of the Act upon an industry which did not welcome the restrictions placed upon it...[he] succeeded in laying the foundations for the reorganisation of this Area of the passenger transport industry and in building up an administrative organisation which has won the confidence of operators. His judgment, scrupulous integrity and desire to administer justice to all who came before him rightly earned for him a position of high esteem in this Area, and the affection with which he was regarded by the operators in this Area was demonstrated by the handsome compliments paid to him on his retirement...'

The Conference of 21 and 22 October 1937 also noted his retirement and he reported the receipt of many appreciative letters and:

> *'He felt that these expressions were not merely personal to himself, but showed the regard in which the work of the Department, and of Commissioners and Licensing Authorities as a body, was held by those who came into direct contact with the licensing systems.'*

The efforts which Colonel Redman and his twelve colleagues had put in over those 7 years were considerable and, within the context that the road passenger industry should be controlled and co-ordinated, successful. It was probably one of the first occasions upon which it is recorded that the industry had come to feel affection for their Commissioners. That was no doubt engendered, to some extent, by the respect in which the Commissioners held the operators and the employees in the industry. The Commissioner for the South Wales Traffic Area made his view quite clear in his Report:

> *'We feel that not only are we justified in saying it but that we ought to say and it is our pleasure to say that in our opinion the standard of everyone engaged in the industry in this Area is particularly high...The feeling between the operators themselves and between the operators and the public is excellent; the drivers and conductors are well behaved and courteous...the utmost good feeling prevails and this not only reduces the work of the Administration, but, and which is far more important, makes the work more pleasant for everyone concerned...'*

They were also concerned about those engaged in working on the buses and in some respects their view were well ahead of their times. The Northern Scotland Commissioner expressed the view that:

> *'The wages paid to female conductors are less than those paid to male conductors and thus the platform costs in such cases are less than in the case of operators...whose staff is male. It would thus appear to be not unreasonable that suitable facilities should be provided at terminal points for the use, comfort and recreation specifically of the female staff...the provision of even a recreation room where some social intercourse might be enjoyed would help to protect female employees from the tendency to become mere units or cogs in the machine...'*

The Commissioner for the Northern Traffic Area was less concerned with flowing lines and air conditioning in public service vehicles, looking to what would become a much more important development in bus design, possibly the inspiration for the eventually ubiquitous Leyland National:

> *'...a new type of four-wheeled vehicle fitted with 40 seats, all of which are facing forward, has been in experimental operation. The engine is mounted*

on the offside of the chassis between the front and rear axles, the former being set well back, giving a large amount of front overhang. The driver sits forward of the front axle, and the entrance door is forward of the front wheel ...The operations of this vehicle have proved a technical and commercial success...'

The North-Western Commissioner noted an improvement, which many bus drivers must have welcomed:

'In many instances, particularly on stage carriages, drivers' seats are now fitted which are adjustable both laterally and vertically...'

One might have thought that drivers of long distance coaches might also have found adjustable seats a benefit. The Commissioner does not comment upon why it should relate particularly to stage carriage operations.

At their Conference on 20 January 1938 the Commissioners were still concerned about the extension of the duration of 'A' and 'B' carriers' licences, which had still not been resolved. But by their Conference on 7 and 8 April 1938 they were beginning to tackle the possibility that there might be a war:

'Mr Browett [who seems to have replaced Sir Cyril and by the next Conference in July 1938 had become Sir Leonard Browett] recommended that the Chairmen should give permission to their staff to join the ARP Units as Air Wardens, etc., but on the definite understanding that, when joining any voluntary organisations, the officers concerned should make it clear, if their own Department required their services in an emergency, it must have prior claim...'

There are some other hints that changes were afoot linked to international affairs. The South Wales Commissioner noted in his Report that there was a continued expansion in the numbers of workmen employed in connection with the various rearmament works in different parts of his area. Unsympathetic Commissioners in the South Eastern Area refused an application for a licence from a new RAF station at Thorney Island to the nearest village (Emsworth) because they did not think the road was good enough. They happily concluded:

'The year to which the present report refers has on the whole been a quiet and uneventful one...'

though they did go on to add the qualification:

'...in the annals of road transport services by road...'

The pace towards war was perhaps speeding up because at their Conference on 20 January 1939 they considered some draft regulations for the emergency use of goods vehicles and were thanked by Sir Leonard for their co-operation in the preparation of the scheme of emergency arrangements. The Civil Defence Act 1939 gave power to the Commissioner of Works to make orders empowering local authorities to take possession of any vehicles, but not without the previous consent of the Traffic Commissioners for the area.[50]

During the War the Commissioners had to set aside their normal functions. From 1940 the Government created the Ministry of War Transport. Within the Ministry was the Defence Transport Council and as part of that were Regional Transport Commissioners. The Regions were not exactly co-extensive with the Traffic Areas but initially each of the Commissioners was appointed to substantially the same area for which he had been responsible in peacetime.[51]

The Commissioners maintained a special involvement with national security well after the War ended, indeed until relatively recently. They became important members of the Regional Emergency Planning Committees. Each Regional Committee, under the Regional Director of the Department of Transport, consisted of in addition to the Commissioner, the Chief Constable(s), Chief Fire Officer, Head of the Ambulance Service, head of emergency services from the Health Service, senior gas and electricity representatives, representative of the Board of Trade and the Army District Commander.

The principal purpose of the Committees was to plan what should happen after a nuclear attack or any civil emergency short of that. The intention was that they should deal with the continuing situation and from his bunker the Commissioner would become the Transport Commissioner. The Traffic Area Offices (presumably if they survived the nuclear attack) were to become Transport Planning Centres and with the vehicle inspectorate were to be responsible for the control of fuel supplies by the issue of vouchers with priority for essential services; requisitioning of vehicles, either by direct contracts for which the operators would be paid, or by direct requisitioning when vehicles, after inspection by a vehicle examiner, would be driven by service personnel. There was no provision for direct labour. At the end of the emergency the vehicles were to be taken to a test station where certificates of condition would be filed before the vehicles were handed back to their owners. They were not concerned with natural disasters.

Brigadier Michael Turner (Traffic Commissioner South Eastern and Metropolitan Traffic Area 1986-1999) recalls being somewhat surprised, on his appointment, to find this was part of the job. By that time the nuclear risk had faded. Nevertheless he found that not only did he have to attend a Committee meeting every six months but that his office staff also had one day of training each year. He considered that by this time the most likely scenario would be a major petrol tanker drivers' strike or other major road strike. There was available a list of Service HGV drivers plus a large number of cooks, clerks and so on as well as a significant number of RAF aircrew. The representative of the Board of Trade had power to freeze fuel stocks, which would only be released against fuel vouchers issued by traffic examiners (all of whom were trained) across the region.

To the best of his knowledge the powers were never used and with the fall of the Berlin Wall the importance began to drop. The remaining functions were handed over to full time civil servants.

Brigadier Turner also recalls that the Wartime powers were extensively used in the build up to D-day. His father, who was in the haulage business, was one who was directed to use his vehicles to carry stores to Weymouth.

It was also a requirement during those years that Commissioners made recommendations for the Honours List.

For a period after the War only summary reports were published. By 1947 the Commissioners had returned to their normal duties only to find that a significant proportion was to be taken away by the Transport Act 1947. Not only that, it took away the title of Commissioners as well, substituting Licensing Authority for Public Service Vehicles (and 'for Goods Vehicles').[52] It was not until paragraph 40 of Schedule 8 the Transport Act 1953 that they regained the dignity of being Traffic Commissioners and reverting to 'Licensing Authority' only when dealing with the goods vehicle side.

8 Nationalisation

The 1947 Transport Act created the British Transport Commission[53] with the powers, inter alia, to carry goods and passengers by road[54] and to acquire by agreement the whole or any part of an undertaking.[55] Of more importance was section 39 which gave compulsory powers to acquire any business (with certain exceptions as to type of carriage) which was predominantly[56] 'long distance', which was defined as being a journey of 40 miles or upwards, measured along the actual route and where the vehicle was carrying goods at some point 25 miles from its operating centre.[57] Vehicles operated by the Commission did not require A or B licences.[58] Unless vehicles were operated under a permit from the Commission they were made subject to a condition preventing the vehicle operating more than 25 miles from its centre when carrying goods.[59]

The Commissioners still had some additional work to do. They became a protective body for those operators who had permits from the Commission. If the Commission wished to revoke them it had to apply to the Commissioners to do so.[60] Also it was not until the end of 1949 early 1950 that they completed the transition of war-time defence certificates to carriers licences.

The Commission was also empowered to prepare 'area road transport schemes' for passenger transport.[61] After consultation the Minister could bring these into effect including the power for a designated operator to acquire an undertaking (or part).[62] Road service licensing did not apply within the area other than to a limited extent in respect of the physical route.[63]

In passing it should be noted that section 72(1) renamed the Railway Rates Tribunal as the Transport Tribunal and transferred the appellate provisions of section 15 of the Road and Rail Transport Act 1933 to it.

In some respects there was little change. The Commissioner for the Northern Traffic Area reported that he had granted 21 'B' licences in substitution for horses and carts and the Metropolitan Commissioner noticed a similar trend which he attributed to the difficulties in 'horse carmen' obtaining suitable vehicles.

1951 was the first year back under a full regimen of 'A' and 'B' licences and the Commissioners must have been just settling down to a predominantly nationalised industry when they were hit by tempest and legislation as they set out in their 1952/3 report. The tempest hit the East Coast:

> *'The urgent repairs made necessary by the extensive damage done to the East Coast sea defences by floods in February, 1953 required the services of a large number of vehicles...the Licensing Authorities concerned with this emergency pay tribute to the vehicle owners for their ready and willing co-operation in providing the necessary road transport at very short notice, and to the drivers of these vehicles, who under extremely adverse conditions never failed to respond to all demands made upon their services...'*

They also had to keep the supplies of margarine going:

> *'Margarine, Edible fats and Welfare Foods. The continued rationing of these margarine and fats necessitated the retention of the war-time arrangements for the stocking and distribution of these commodities...Special authorisations...were issued to permit the continuation of this traffic but the need for these will cease with the withdrawal of rationing restrictions in 1954...'*

Of rather more long-term effect was the Transport Act 1953 which provided for the de-nationalisation of some 90% of the British Transport Commission's holdings. It was required to dispose of its holdings 'as quickly as reasonably possible'[64] by sale by public tender with the benefit of a free five-year 'A' licence.[65] The Commission's vehicles came back under carriers' licensing and the statutory 25-mile limit came to an end.[66] A further easing of the position of would be hauliers and expanding haulage businesses was the shifting of the onus to the objector.[67] Passenger transport facilities were also brought back under the control of the Commissioners and the Road Traffic Act 1930.[68]

A Commissioner who had sat in 1939 would have found that over-all there had been little change. The Road Traffic Act 1956 increased the disciplinary powers of the Commissioners under the 1933 Act[69] and redefined various terms in the 1930 Act.[70]

The next big event for the Commissioners was the oil crisis of May 1957, not the last they would have to deal with. They were responsible for the rationing of motor fuel used by commercial vehicles which they complained led to the temporary dislocation of licensing and a complete cessation of enforcement work.

Coming over the horizon was the Road Traffic Act 1960 which consolidated, with only very minor changes, the legislation from 1930 onwards. The terms of appointment of Traffic Commissioners remained the same as did the eleven traffic areas.[71] Apart from having to memorise a few different section numbers there was no great change for the Commissioners.

The Yorkshire Licensing Authority in his 1959/60 Report made a complaint which was to be repeated many times across the traffic areas until the abolition of carriers' licensing and later road service licensing:

> *'Despite much publicity in the Traffic Court and the trade press, many applicants for licences still fail to attend Public Inquiries for which their cases have been listed and thus waste the time of advocates, witnesses, objectors and official shorthand writers. In some cases it is the objectors who do not attend. One recent example concerned an application in respect of which 30 objections had been received. When the case was called, it was found that although their legal representative was present, none of the objectors...had troubled to put in an appearance...'*

This was against a background of considerable conflict over applications for 'A' and 'B' licences:

> *'The BTC [British Transport Commission] continue to be very active in lodging objections to the applications of independent road operators, who in turn are also showing a lively interest in the applications of other operators generally...'*

At this time the West Midland Traffic Area was still holding as many as 143 Public Sittings a year to deal with road haulage matters. The Licensing authority noted the beginning of the impact of the major road-building programme:

> *'Many operators are making use of the new Motor Road and as a result their vehicles have been much more likely to be affected by breakdowns. These were due mainly to over-heating, tyre failures, lack of fuel, broken fan belts, and engine failures caused by higher speeds being maintained over longer distances... some drivers have been slow in adapting their standards to meet intelligently the challenge of the new Motor Way...' [i.e. the M1 motorway]*

and noted:

> *'There was pressure on transport for the pea harvest...'*

Not only did the volume of work required of the Traffic Commissions vary with changes in the law but they could also vary because of local circumstances to a very marked degree. The Report gives a particular instance in the South Wales Traffic Area:

> *'During the year, the preparation of the site and approach roads for the new steel works at Llanwern involved the movement of approximately 7½ million*

cubic yards of shale...At the peak period up to 1000 vehicles were engaged on this work...in all 1,774 short term licences...were issued during the year...there was also a constant change of vehicles and nearly 3,000 vehicle identification certificates were issued...'

This huge civil engineering undertaking also impacted on the Western Traffic Area:

'Lorries came from all over the country in response to advertisements in the Press. Large numbers were put to use without their owners' troubling to obtain the necessary carriers licences...'

The Licensing Authority also noted an area of competition that must have made for interesting even if malodorous public sittings:

'...[a] field of endeavour that evokes considerable objection is the provision of additional facilities for the clearing of cesspools and the removal of waste substances from garages and slaughterhouses. The jealousy amongst the providers of these facilities is most marked and it is generally necessary to set aside at least one whole day for the hearing on any application...'

Frequently, Commissioners were dismayed at the lenient treatment of offenders convicted of offences under the various Acts and regulations that they were charged with enforcing, but sometimes they were quite pleased with the outcomes:

'...a Weymouth operator who faced eleven charges of breach of licence conditions and nine charges of failing to cause records to be kept. He was fined over £300 with costs. One director and one of the drivers were also committed to stand trial at Dorset Assizes on charges of perjury when fines and costs totalling £575 were imposed. In the Weymouth case the records triggered off an investigation; underestimating the intelligence of the examiner, those responsible falsely declared the carriage of brick from Salisbury...whereas it is known that wherever bricks are produced it is not in Salisbury...'

Then as now they could find the Transport Tribunal somewhat frustrating as an appeal body. In his 1960/61 Report the Licensing Authority for the Northern Traffic Area commented on two cases (probably through gritted teeth):

'I refused to renew the A licence of a known criminal serving a sentence of three years' imprisonment for receiving, and who had used a specified vehicle for the carriage of stolen goods...His appeal was allowed by the Transport Tribunal, a licence was granted to him on his discharge from prison...'

'A 'C' licence holder used a specified vehicle to carry away £2,700 worth of goods stolen by him by warehouse breaking. The goods were not recovered

and I revoked the licence on the basis that the vehicle must have been used for the purpose of reward...The Transport Tribunal allowed the appeal, and a licence was granted to this man on his discharge from prison...'

He probably was not pleased when the law as it stood required him to deal with another case in a particular way:

'At Carlisle...a "haulage contractor" was caught warehouse breaking and later sentenced to eight years preventative detention. I previously refused to renew this man's A licence...he merely formed a Limited Company for his wife which enabled him to continue his career...'

The Western Area Licensing Authority continued his interest in reporting on somewhat esoteric types of road haulage:

'Armoured vehicles, hitherto employed for warlike purposes or for the protection of dictators are now being used to counter the pay-roll robbers. Licences have been granted to three firms specialising in this work ...'

And he had a warning for those seeking an apparently easy way into the industry:

'The demand for tipping lorries brings its own problems...The...move is for the quarry owners to obtain 'C' hiring allowances, and employ the unlicensed lorries of the angry young men [who have had their applications for 'B' licences refused] *under 'C' licence. The time of reckoning comes when the job is over – sometimes after a week or two – and the chastened vehicle owners either abandon the attempt or chase round for other 'C' hiring work...the back door entry leads more often than not to pitiable results...'*

9 No easy access

There was no easy entry to road haulage. The law contained no provision for the transfer of either 'A' or 'B' licences. Despite the fact that, over the years, the practice had grown up of 'buying' and 'selling' licences. An 'A' licence had a recognised value per ton. The 'purchaser' could either apply for a licence in respect of the unexpired portion of the 'vendor's' licence and for the actual vehicles covered or a new licence. In the former case the Licensing Authority had discretion not to publish notice of the application and to grant it. That he might do if he was satisfied that the 'purchaser' was simply stepping into the shoes of the 'vendor' and that there was a 'live' business. There was no automatic entitlement and, despite over twenty five years having passed since the 1933 Act, the Licensing Authority for the Metropolitan Traffic Area thought it expedient to issue a warning:

> *'The misconception is still widespread that licences are themselves negotiable and that when buying vehicles with licences, it follows that the purchaser will automatically obtain a licence. This misunderstanding sometimes has unfortunate consequences for the purchaser who subsequently finds that he is unable to support his application by adequate evidence [that there is a "live" haulage business]...'*

There were still one or two Steptoe & Sons in business but the Metropolitan licensing authority noted in his report for 1961-2 what was probably one of the last applications taking advantage of section 174(4)(e) of the Transport Act 1960, which gave favourable treatment to a haulier wishing to change to motorised transport:

> *'During the year only one application was received from a carrier who sought to substitute motor vehicles for horse-drawn transport and a 'B' licence authorising two vehicles was granted...'*

This device did not provide an easy access to the industry because a 'B' licence was only granted for the same carrying capacity as the horses and carts and for a similar radius to that assumed for a horse, normally 15 miles.[72]

Applications to increase fares became both more frequent and more contentious during the 1960s and remained so until fares conditions were abolished by the Transport Act 1980. In the West Midland Traffic Area the Commissioners dealt with an application by the Birmingham and Midland Motor Omnibus Co Ltd that attracted objections from 20 local authorities. They granted fare increases as follows:

'Fares up to 1/11½d to be increased by not more than 1d
2/- to 4/11d to be increased by not more than 2d
5/- to 7/11d – by not more than 3d
8/- and over by not more than 6d.'

The East Midland Traffic Area dealt with nineteen applications for increases of which five were from municipal undertakings.

In the same period the Commissioners began to note that the shortage of drivers and conductors was beginning to cause serious problems for operators. In the Northern Traffic Area:

'The Municipal undertakings and large bus companies still report a shortage of drivers and conductors...'

The position in the Western Traffic Areas was no better:

'...the shortage of drivers and conductors is still serious. The Devon General Omnibus and Touring Company Ltd, for instance, arranged to interview in Belfast applicants for employment as conductors...'

'...in consequence we had more applications than usual for public service vehicle drivers' licences from men with unsatisfactory medical histories involving coronary thrombosis, diabetes, epilepsy, cerebra-vascular disease, multiple sclerosis and valvular disease of the heart...'

The Commissioners were always interested to note developments in the industry. It is difficult to get too excited about developments in the North-Western Traffic Area:

'...applications for sightseeing excursions along the new M6 motorway were granted...'

1960/61 saw the first appearances of a new pressure group before the Commissioners for the Northern Traffic Area, which eventually, after a number of more years campaigning succeeded in its aims:

'The National Society of Non-smokers made representations to us that smoking should be banned on the lower deck of double decked vehicles, and lodged

objections when certain road service licences held by a large bus company came up for renewal. We heard the Society's representations at a Public sitting, but decided they had not produced sufficient evidence for smoking to be banned upon lower decks...'

They were back again the next year:

'...representations were made by a number of local authorities and other bodies that smoking should be banned on the lower decks of double decked vehicles. We again took the matter up with some of the larger bus companies and they agreed to exhibit notices on lower decks 'requesting' the public to refrain from smoking...'

1961 and 1962 were years in which the Commissioners dealt with some novel applications for road service licences which also reflected considerable social change because of immigration. The East Midland Commissioner reported:

'...[that] *bus operators can still spread their wings is indicated by 2 recent applications. One by Barton Transport for an express carriage service between Nottingham, Harwich and Warsaw, and the other by an as yet unestablished small operator who was seeking among other ambitious proposals, an express carriage service between Nottingham, Dover, Calcutta and Singapore...'*

The next year the Yorkshire Commissioners were not to be out done:

'During March an application was received for a road service licence for a service of express carriage between Bradford and Pakistan: picking up and setting down passengers at Bradford, Sheffield Birmingham and London. The vehicle will embark at Dover and travel overland from Calais to Karachi and Lahore. It is proposed to leave Bradford on the first day of each month and arrive at Karachi in 16 or 17 days...'

Unfortunately the Commissioners did not report whether any coach ever departed let alone arrived. It seems likely that a rather more modest proposal in the same Traffic Area would have been successful:

'A short period licence was granted to a Pakistani to operate a service between Bradford and London Airport via Huddersfield and Birmingham. This facility was to enable him to carry his fellow countrymen from the West Riding to the airport to enable them to meet relatives arriving from Pakistan...'

There were no such exotic applications in the North-Western Traffic Area but they did record, in the same year, a new form of passenger transport:

'...one interesting application which has recently been received, is for an excursion to North Wales via Hoylake. It is intended that the passengers should travel from Hoylake to Rhyl by hovercraft, while the coach runs light to Rhyl to resume the road excursion...'

The Commissioners in the Western Traffic Area were somewhat bemused by an application for a road service licence for a hovercraft:

> 'An *application by another operator to run a hovercraft from another base in Cornwall was referred to the Air Transport Licensing Board but* [he was advised] *that future legislation might require him to apply to us for a licence if he intended to hover for hire or reward along or over a road...'*

I do not think that any such legislation was passed and I recall that in the case of a fatal accident involving a hovercraft it was indeed treated as an aeroplane and investigated as an air accident.

West Midland residents were it seems rather more adventurous, the Commissioners noting in relation to extended tours to the Continent:

> *'...activity in this field has increased – the most noteworthy development being the use of air transport for the Channel crossing. The flight ranges between a mere 'hop' across the Channel to one ending 300 miles or more into Europe. Not only is the flight itself providing an added attraction but it enables either a longer stay to be made at the continental holiday centre or opens up new territory for the touring holiday proper...'*

A recurring theme from this time onwards, and one which is still there today, is the loss of rural bus services. Operators could not simply cease to operate but needed to apply to the Commissioners who, often faced with objections to the loss of a service, had nevertheless to look at reality as the Western Area Commissioners pointed out:

> *'...a bus service taken off was a circular 6 mile service which ran twice on Saturdays only. During the period of 6 weeks before it was taken off only one passenger was carried, once at a single fare and once on a return ticket. The total receipts during the 6 weeks amounted to 2/-. There can be no justification for asking an operator to continue such a service...'*

10 Touching faith

Many operators had, over the 30 years of the Commissioners, developed a touching faith in their powers and their preparedness to become involved, at least on behalf of the small operator. The Western Commissioners could not resist providing in full a cry from the heart of one small operator who had bought a pig in a poke:

'Having run this stage service since last May up to 31 December I have analysed the mileage and passengers. I enclose the figures, they work out as follows.

Number of passengers carried – 4328
Number of miles travelled – 4505
Total fares taken – £228

This works out at about 1/- per mile. This is not sufficient to maintain the service. With no excursion or tours licences to support it, we cannot go on at a constant loss.

Having paid for petrol and wages, we were left with a credit balance of £4 for tax, insurance, capital depreciation, wear and tear and maintenance of vehicles. Quite impossible! We have written to the county council to ask if they would consider a subsidy to maintain this rural service. We await their reply.

Also we have asked 6 other local operators who are better off than us, having either stage services or tours to support them, if they are interested in buying the licence. Only two operators have replied saying they do not want it. So being faced with being unable to dispose of the licence by sale, and not having a bank balance big enough to face a yearly loss it is quite impossible.

The suspension will have to be quite soon, in 4 to 5 weeks time, at the latest, because by that time there will be no money left for petrol to run it any way!

It would not pay anyone further afield to try and run it because due to dead mileage to and from the starting and finishing places. Perhaps you would ask the operators concerned if they are interested in this licence (if you have not already done so). There are those about who would refuse to purchase from us to obtain the licence free when we have to stop. We had to pay £250 for it. We would like our money back.

For the moment we have no set date for ceasing to operate. First we will give the public 4 weeks notice to the effect that we are to close down; this will only be after we have had good time allowed for sale of licence, or the County Council have finally turned down our application to support the service along this route. Should you in the meantime find a buyer at £250, what we had to pay, then OK, we will pass it on.

Can we be granted a suspension for a period to jerk the county council into activity one way or the other? All the while the bus runs at a loss or otherwise no one will bother about it at all.'

In 1962 Colonel A S Redmond, the original Chairman of the Traffic Commissioners for the West Midland Traffic Area died, having retired on 31 December 1937. The then present incumbent, Mr John Else, wrote of him:

'...his judgement, scrupulous integrity and desire to administer justice to all who came before him rightly earned for him a position of high esteem in this Area...'

Some of us will remember the severe winter of 1962/3. Most Commissioners commented on it including the North-Western Commissioner:

'The exceptionally severe winter resulted in a substantial increase in the number of short-term licences granted for the carriage of coal and fuel. These were granted initially for a period of one month...It was found that even in these extreme conditions the licensing system was flexible enough to cope adequately with the situation ...'

and the Eastern:

'...the severe weather conditions necessitated a few exceptional movements such as the movement by road of fuel and grain from Great Yarmouth to Norwich, which would normally have gone by river, and the provision of vehicles to convey water to outlying villages...'

The Western Commissioners were intrigued with steps taken by Bristol Omnibus to improve the recruitment and training of drivers, anticipating by many years the use of video games:

> *'...to assist the training of PSV drivers the Company purchased and installed a training machine in August 1962. This consists of a projection assembly presenting a simulated moving roadway to the trainee who 'drives a double decked bus mock-up' which itself remains stationary, the accuracy of the steering and gear changes is reflected in an illuminated screen in front of the driver...'*

Whilst the Commissioners routinely reported on road checks and maintenance of vehicles only rarely did they go into any detail. The 1963/4 Report was the last for Mr S W Nelson (after 16 years in the post) of the Western Traffic Area and both as Commissioner and Licensing Authority he allowed himself to be amused:

> *'An owner, who happened to be a passenger in his own vehicle which was stopped for excessive smoke, hotly contested the examiner's view and denied that the vehicle was smoking. He was persuaded to alight and to direct the vehicle, by a detour, to approach the checkpoint again. After the vehicle's departure the lorry owner became an enthusiastic observer and soon pointed out a vehicle in the distance which he considered was a 'real smoker' and asked what the examiner was going to do about it. There was no need to do anything about it as it had already been done. It was the owner's vehicle returning...'*

He returned to the problem of loss of rural bus services:

> *'Widecombe-in-the-Moor has been threatened with the breakdown which occurred in the days of Tom Pearce who originally supplied the necessary horse transport in the district. He was succeeded by a lady who ran the service with a pony and trap. She in her turn had handed over the reins to her young grand daughter who 40 years ago changed over to motor buses. Now that the descendants of Bill Brewer, Jan Stewer and the rest have got themselves cars, the decline in traffic has forced this company to give up business after suffering serious and increasing losses in the last few years. The company had applied for authority to reduce the service but this proposal drew objection from the local authority. This seems to have been the last straw and the company felt they had no option but to terminate the service, a serious matter for the local inhabitants who have thus been left without any public transport...'*

Despite his many years in office he was clearly not averse to modern developments in modes of transport:

'Clovelly is a picturesque and popular holiday resort – very well known for its steep cobbled high street which is closed to vehicles. It is one thing to descend to the harbour on foot but quite another for tired pedestrians to climb up again by the 1:3½ gradient back road from the village. We have licensed a service on this road by 7-seater vehicles of the Land Rover type with 4-wheel drive and reduction gearing which are said to be the only vehicles suitable for such service...'

The Western Commissioners' view of the countryside was perhaps a little different from that of the North-Western Commissioners:

'...all who travel on M6 cannot but agree that it is a very attractive and welcome addition to the road system and that its benefits should be used to the full...'

The Commissioners had two areas with which they suffered continual frustration and frequently commented upon it. The first was that magistrates did not impose realistic penalties when they brought prosecutions either in relation to buses or lorries. The East Midland Commissioners could not help commenting on one case:

'...the...case involved the prosecution of a psv operator carrying 18 passengers in excess of the 44 permitted on a single decked coach. Although a conviction was obtained, the driver of the coach was fined only 10/- and the operator £1 and costs were refused...'

The second area was that of unlicensed operation under cover of a pretence that the passengers were a private party not travelling at separate fares, the operator therefore not requiring a road service licence. The operations were frequently of workers travelling to their places of work (later to bingo halls and other places of entertainment). The frustration was more keenly felt by licensed operators who were losing large amounts of potential passenger revenue. The Commissioners noted the endeavours of one South Wales company to tackle the problem (and in the days before video cameras):

'One company...filmed the activities of some of these mini-bus operators... In company with other interested parties we were invited to attend a private showing of the film. We were very impressed and were left without any doubt in our minds as to the extent of this apparently illegal operation and found it impossible to believe that the passengers travelling on these vehicles were doing so without payment. We [are] of the opinion that a great deal of good will ensue if this film were shown to a wider audience...'

By the mid-1960s the general stability that had existed in bus fares had come to an end. In the 1964/5 Report the Commissioners for the Northern Traffic Area were sad to note an application by Middlesborough:

'...[the] Corporation have had a minimum 1d fare since horse drawn trams started in 1874, being the only town in the country to retain it. We are sure it is with regret that the council has decided to apply for that 1d fare to be abolished. The passing of this 1d fare is equally regretted by your Commissioners...'

An annual application in the late spring or early summer was becoming the norm as platform staff gained increases in wages in a round that generally applied from April. Some traffic areas found that two applications had been made during the twelve months. The Western Commissioners reported:

'...the most significant feature of the second round of applications has been the attempt by most large operators to fix a 4d minimum fare. This has so far been resisted and we have retained a 3d fare for reduced mileage which we feel will be of great benefit to the elderly and infirm whose need to take a bus for short distances is the greatest...'

There was some alleviation in due course for the elderly because of the Travel Concessions Act 1964 but annual or bi-annual fares applications become the norm until fares conditions were removed by the Transport Act 1980. These applications became a major element in the work of the Commissioners. Most applications were opposed by local authorities and were hotly contested. The normal pattern was of applications by the major NBC companies and the Municipals with the smaller operators making 'coming into line applications'. That is, their fares were brought into line with the larger companies where there were common lengths of route. Whilst the approach was generally to the financial benefit of the smaller operators, the rationale was to prevent abstraction of passengers from the larger operator, which would otherwise have higher fares. Whilst the 'coming into line' applications were generally not opposed the major applications often lasted two or more days. There were not infrequent appeals to the Minister either by unsuccessful applicants or unsuccessful objectors.

The same Report commented upon another problem of which the Commissioners were becoming more and more aware, and to which they were sympathetic when operators suspended services, that of hooliganism on buses. The Northern Commissioners recorded:

'...assaults on bus crews have led to the withdrawal of Sunday night buses as a warning to the public...one authority is to fit alarm systems on its buses to give warning to police if conductors are attacked. Hooliganism generally makes the operator's task most difficult...'

and in the Eastern Area:

'...the Saturday evening express service was discontinued because of continued vandalism by passengers returning from dances...'

The opening up of the motorways and other road improvements were leading to new excursions and tours. The Yorkshire Commissioners were having great difficulty in understanding the travelling public's enthusiasm (or masochism):

'...most of these excursions involve a return journey of 400 miles. To many it may seem that a certain proportion of day excursionists are 'devils for punishment', but nevertheless the returns from operators show that there is a certain type of day excursionist who really does enjoy a day trip starting at 0645 hours and returning at 2400 hours...'

The 1965/6 Report seems to record the first woman to be appointed a Commissioner. (It was to be well over 30 years before a female full-time Commissioner was appointed.) Councillor Mrs. M Blower is noted as one of the Commissioners for the Eastern Traffic Area, where rural bus services were continuing to be a problem for the Commissioners:

'... the pruning of services has continued. During the year we have found that even those country bus operators, whose services originated in the days of the village carrier and whose operations are still very local, have begun to apply to withdraw facilities which they seem to have been providing, at all events in recent years, largely from a sense of local responsibility and good neighbourliness...'

Whilst the Commissioners had their specific jurisdiction in relation to fares they were also required to give effect to national policy. The prices and incomes standstill came into effect on 20 July 1966 under the Prices and Incomes Act 1966. As a result in the year covered by the 1966/7 Reports there were few fares applications, most operators having to postpone any proposals until July 1967.

The North-Western Commissioners noted a new approach to the planning of bus services which was being pioneered by Wallasey Corporation:

'...having taken a unique step by engaging a firm of business research consultants to plan, with the aid of a computer, a complete re-organisation of their services in the light of current need...'

Later more and more companies adopted similar projects generally described as market analysis projects (MAPs) leading to major re-organisations of bus services. The West Midland Commissioners saw that the writing was on the wall for traditional bus services unless there were significant changes:

'...the substantial body of well informed opinion which considers that the vast majority of persons now using stage carriage services do so because no

alternative form of transport, public or private, is available to them, the Commissioners consider that that day is not far distant [when the public use will decline greatly]...Unless before it dawns public road transport facilities have improved e.g. by giving it traffic priority and costs have been lowered...on a hitherto unconsidered scale, the Commissioners believe that the industry will have to be subsidised either nationally and/or locally if it is to maintain the level of service necessary and desirable in the public interest...'

The Commissioner for that Area also commented on the state of the road haulage industry:

'Whilst licensing continues to follow its well established pattern I am conscious of a lack of buoyancy and an air of caution in both the public and private sectors of the haulage industry. I suspect that this reflects the restraints imposed on the national economy and uncertainty about the shape and effect of future goods vehicle licensing...'

Traffic Commissioners 1931

Aldwych–Beaconsfield service began 27 February 1931

Traffic Commissioners 1974
Back row, left to right: Sheridan, Birnie, Thornton, Crabtree, Jackson, Robson
Front row, left to right: Potter, Hodgson,Robertson, Hanlon, Elmslie

Traffic Commissioners 2005
Back row, left to right: Dixon, Brown, Simms
Front row, left to right: Macartney, Aitken, Bell, Heaps

North Western Commissioners 1948-1999

Williamson 1948-1962

Elmslie 1962-1965

Hodgson 1965-1975

Hutchings 1975-1987

Albu 1987-1995

Waterworth 1996-1999

Picture supplied courtesy of Gerald Sharp Photography

Upholding a transport tradition.
Christopher Heaps, as Commissioner for the City marks a coach at the annual cart marking ceremony of the Worshipful Company of Carmen, Guildhall Yard 2005.

The author in conversation with Ronald Jackson, one of the longest serving Commissioners.

Two of the earliest vehicles to come under the watchful eye of the Traffic Commissioners.

The West Midlands Traffic Commissioners 1968
Left to right: Fullwood, Else (Chairman), Foster
Bertram Foster was later Commissioner Northern Traffic Area

Philip Brown MA LLB FCILT
Senior Traffic Commissioner for Great Britain & Commissioner Western

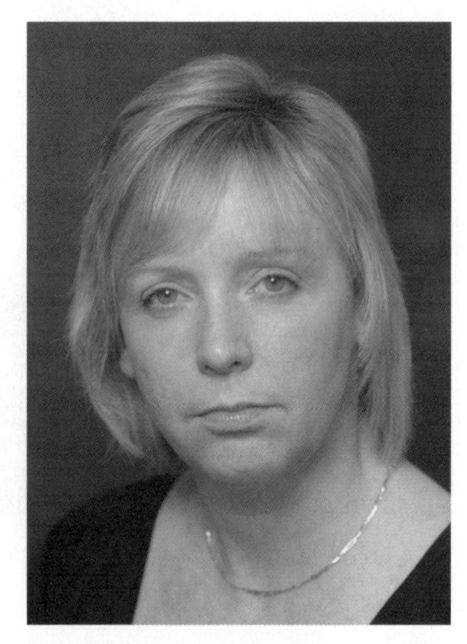

Beverley Bell LLB FCILT
Commissioner North Western and first full-time female Commissioner

Traffic Commissioners at Lancaster House, 1974

A typical long distance 'A' licensed haulage vehicle – 1935 AEC Mammoth Major MkII. (© T. Monckton)

Own-account operated 1946 Dennis Pax 5-tonner on 'C' licence. (© P Sposito)

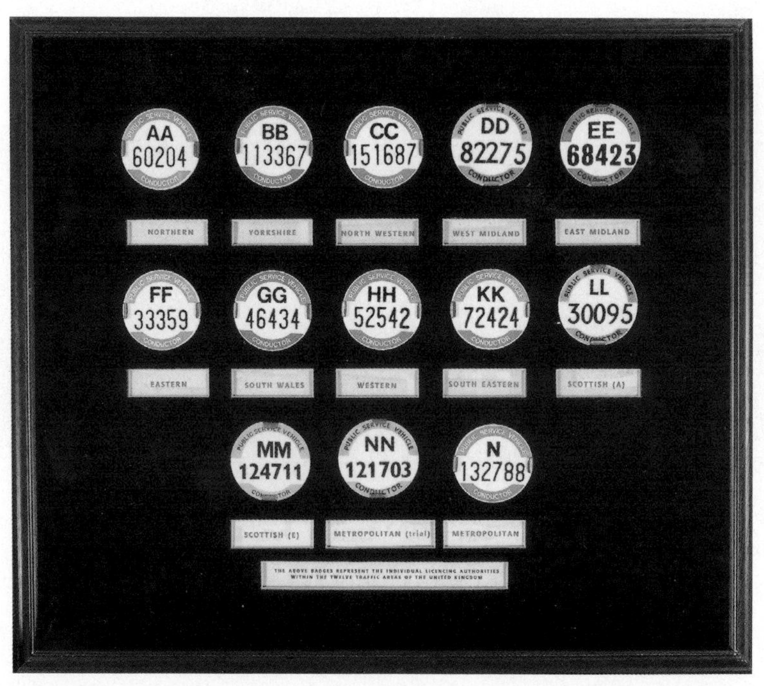

Display of Traffic Area psv conductors' badges. (Courtesy Chris Salaman)

11 The Geddes Report

The reference to uncertainty was no doubt to the recommendations of the Geddes Committee on Carrier Licensing that had been published in 1965. The principal recommendation had been the abolition of quantity licensing in the introduction of a stricter system of quality control. The shape at least was soon to come in the Transport Act 1968. Whilst that Act was in due course to make entry to road haulage easier, not all Commissioners liked to see newcomers to passenger transport, particularly in the Northern Area, as was made clear in the 1967/8 Report:

> *'At present any "enthusiastic amateur" or "part timer" may acquire a coach and may enter into wasteful competition with operators established in private hire and contract work as well as those who hold road service licences...In the last two years in this Traffic Area alone there have been no less than 70 new entrants into the industry. The passenger transport industry, as well as the public as a whole, can ill-afford such unlimited infiltration...'*

This gave perhaps an over-simplified view of the difficulties of entering or expanding in the passenger transport industry. Commissioners were faced with public sittings lasting days and sometimes weeks as the major operators sought to increase their share of the market. Some of the biggest battles involved Wallace Arnold often represented by their then chairman Sir Frank Marshall. It did not help that the Commissioners failed to agree, especially when the parties had mistakenly agreed to sit with only two Commissioners as occurred in the North-Western Traffic Area:

> *'What must surely be one of the longest cases ever considered in this Area resulted from applications first submitted in 1966 by Wallace Arnold Tours... to revive their British tours...not operated since 1958. Strong opposition was encountered from practically every tour and long distance express operator in the north-west. After a public sitting taking seven days...I and my fellow*

Commissioner were unable to agree on our decision and the applications were put aside for rehearing at a later date...the Deputy Chairman and two other Commissioners heard the case on eight days...The grant, which was a majority decision, restricted the area from which passengers could be carried...[and] we were not prepared to grant an open licence for the continent...'

Another element of the same battle was being fought out in the Metropolitan Traffic Area:

'*An application to provide the road service for new extended tours in Great Britain has met with considerable opposition. There are eighteen objectors and so far the sitting has lasted 6 days. A further 6 days have been allocated for the case...*'

The Commissioner also had an apparently much more mundane problems, that of the terminus for many South London services:

'*...A third terminal working problem which caused me great concern is at Crystal Palace Parade where eleven services terminate. Buses have for many years carried out a 'U' turning movement on the wide, straight road but with the continuing increase in traffic there have been a number of accidents involving turning buses...Loss of the terminal at Crystal Palace would have a major effect on the* [London Transport] *Board's services in South London...*'

Because of their powers to impose conditions on where passengers might be picked up and set down the Commissioners were frequently involved in disputes over bus stops having to attend many site visits. Residents rarely wanted bus stops outside their own houses but equally did not want the stops to be very far away. They must frequently have exercised the judgement of Solomon.

Whilst the Transport Act 1962 had little impact on the Commissioners, its principal purpose being to bring to an end the British Transport Commission, devolving its powers to various boards as public authorities[73] the Transport Act 1968 completely recast the licensing of goods vehicles to a quality based system,[74] provided for transport managers' licences,[75] and created the National Freight Corporation.[76]

On the passenger side the Act created The National Bus Company and the Scottish Transport Group transferring to them all large non-municipal bus operators.[77] Whilst this may have had little impact on the Commissioners, the creation of Passenger Transport Authorities and Passenger Transport Executives did. The PTAs and PTEs were given very wide powers within their designated areas to carry passengers, though the requirement that they would not require road service licences was not implemented.[78] However the Commissioners had to take into account representations made by a PTE when granting road service licences or backings.[79]

Over the next three years the Commissioners dealt with the transition from carriers' licensing to operators' licensing. The Act also saw the introduction of the licensing of heavy goods vehicle drivers, another responsibility which fell to the Commissioner. At least on this occasion they were not faced with quite the sudden transition with which their predecessors had had to deal under the 1930 and 1933 Acts.

The Commissioners generally seem to have adopted a stoical approach to the changes to a system which, however complicated, had operated for over 30 years. As the West Midland Commissioner said:

> *'I take the view that it is better to travel hopefully, though it be Pilgrim's Progress, than not to travel at all...'*

And the Western Commissioner probably said much the same thing:

> *'The year covered by this report has been one of transition. Tempora mutantur, nos et mutamur in illis...'* [Times change and we change with them – *Harrison's Description of Britain* 1577]

Whilst changes in the law generally created extra work for the Commissioners, the 1968 Act in particular, for example, reduced the jurisdiction of the West Midland Commissioners by the creation of the West Midlands Passenger Transport Authority with effect from 1 April 1969. This Authority had the control of stage and express services (other than excursions and tours). The Commissioners expressed concern for those operators, such as Midland Red, which had services both within and outside the area of the Authority.

Whilst they were beginning to deal with those changes it was business as usual on the passenger side. Fares increases were back in the news. The North-Western Commissioners dealt with 25 applications in the reporting year 1968/9 and the Yorkshire Commissioners commented:

> *'Fifteen applications for fares increases were lodged during the year of which four were from municipal undertakings. All were granted in full or with modifications...The constant round of applications for fares increases is the cause of our greatest concern...we must expect to be faced with continued applications for fares increases...'*

From time to time the Commissioners commented on tragedies which had occurred in their areas and which to some extent fell within their responsibilities. The Yorkshire Commissioners noted one such event:

> *'At the request of the Coroner we were represented at an inquest on a boy who was fatally injured by a public service vehicle. It transpired that the driver of the vehicle was a diabetic and medical evidence was to the effect that the driver could have been suffering from a hypoglycaemic attack...We subsequently revoked his licence...'*

The Scottish Commissioners reverted to the long-term problem of hooliganism on buses and one very sad case indeed:

> *'A deplorable feature is the increasing number of assaults on bus crews, particularly on late night buses at weekends. Matters came to a head in February 1969 when a Glasgow Corporation conductor was attacked and stabbed on his vehicle by a number of youths. He died of his injuries a few days later...'*

The next year the Northern Commissioners reported an even more serious incident:

> *'The most serious crash ever recorded in the North occurred on Crawleyside Bank...on 15 August 1969, causing the deaths of 20 elderly people on a private party outing. Your Commissioners held an Inquiry into the maintenance facilities of the operator concerned and as a result his public service vehicle licence was revoked...'*

By the time of the 1969/70 Report the Commissioners were well underway with the transition to 'O' licensing. The Yorkshire Commissioner emphasised the change that was taking place:

> *'Basically we are faced with a new concept of licensing in which the emphasis is on road safety and in which the condition of the applicants' vehicles and the facilities and arrangements for their maintenance are all important...'*

He also found that:

> *'...there have been many problems and a large proportion of the applications have had to be referred back to the operators for clarification or amendment... the number of former carriers' licence holders who failed to return the application forms sent out prior to each phase was considerable...In the event the shortfall was something of a blessing inasmuch as it helped to keep the work load within manageable bounds...'*

The Northern Commissioner was the one who seemed to have things under control:

> *'The transition to Operators' Licensing is progressing smoothly...'*

The Western Commissioner was only just coping:

> *'...the task of writing within the allotted time the many thousands of vehicle discs needed could not have been completed but for the fact that large numbers of my staff, including my clerk and his executive and clerical officers of all grades, personally wrote as volunteers many such discs in order to give much needed help to those of the troops who were in the front line throughout the battle...'*

I think there would have been few operators who would have agreed with the West Midland Commissioner, though they would have been wise to note his warning:

> *'Undoubtedly there will be those who say there has been too little disciplinary action during the year under report. My answer to this is that in the national interest including that of the transport industry it was essential for the introduction of the new licensing system to be given priority. For the future it may well be that the words of Thomas Gray will prove to be appropriate,*
>
> *Alas regardless of their doom*
> *The little victims play*
> *No sense have they of ills to come*
> *No care beyond today.'*

Having seen the effects of strikes affecting the air transport industry in 2005 it is interesting to note out of what apparently minor situations strikes can be generated. The frustration of the Scottish Commissioner comes out in his report:

> *'In November 1969, a dispute over the position of indicator board winding handles in the Kirkcaldy depot of W Alexander and Sons (Fife) Ltd spread to nearly all of the company's depots in Fife.... Conductresses went on strike in early November...In January 1970, both drivers and conductors went on unofficial strike at all the company's depots. By early March the strike had spread to other companies in Southern Scotland and was causing widespread transport difficulties from Perthshire to the Borders...services were resumed on 27 March...'*

The 1971/2 Report shows that when they were disenchanted with the effects of a piece of legislation they were quite prepared to say so. The West Midland Commissioner was certainly disenchanted with some of the effects of the Transport Act 1968:

> *'After three years the public may be excused when they ask what has been gained by the creation of the* [West Midland Passenger Transport] *Authority and its Executive...Certainly no improvement has been apparent to the public for service frequencies in the main have been curtailed and fares have risen three times...The only persons who appear to have received any tangible benefits are the employees who have achieved wages and conditions of service second to none in the industry...the Commissioners...are beginning to wonder if the Authority/Executive are not following a policy of hastening too slowly...'*

The Metropolitan Commissioner took a lighter view of the year's business:

> '...[an application] *by Samuelson New Transport Company Ltd...to provide meals on wheels for the delectation of tourists...with which J Lyons & Co Ltd were associated was unopposed and granted. It was designed to attract tourists who were willing to pay £10 for a tour of London, a substantial meal and appropriate refreshment to be consumed en route. We have been told that there were few takers and that the vehicle is now up for sale...It has been...a bad year for gimmicks...*'

It was also the year that British Leyland started production of the Leyland National, with the Northern Commissioner noting that the first one had rolled off the production line in Whitehaven and been certified in February 1972.

Rarely did Commissioners ruminate in their annual reports but in his report for 1970/71 the West Midlands Commissioner indulged himself:

> '*The Rail and Road Traffic Act 1933 established a system of quantity licensing ...With some temporary vicissitudes, ie the war years and nationalisation, Carriers' licensing survived almost unchanged till 1969 though the Transport Act of 1953 did ease the criteria for entry into public haulage. The licensing system also provided some not particularly effective safeguard against the use of unsafe vehicles.*
>
> *From its inception until the outbreak of war the licensing system operated primarily as a protection system for the railway companies. Indeed between September 1935 and June 1938 the number of vehicles licensed for public haulage fell by 5% from 156,000 to 148,000. This reflected not only the depression years of the mid-thirties but also that the road haulage industry consisting in the main of small independent units was ill-equipped to meet the highly organised objecting forces of the railway companies.*
>
> *During the war years licensing was replaced by a system of "defence permits". This coupled with fuel rationing and other emergency powers gave the Government through the Licensing Authorities almost complete control of the nature and extent of road transport.*
>
> *Licensing was restored in the second half of 1946 but...it was overtaken by the Transport Act 1947 which placed long distance public haulage and the railways in public ownership...Public haulage outside a 35 (sic) -mile radius could only be undertaken with a permit granted by the* [British Transport] *Commission...*
>
> *In part nationalisation was intended to protect railways from the competition of a rapidly expanding road haulage industry. That it did not operate in this way is not surprising. The railways had been worked to death during the war years ... the pace and form of this expansion [of trade and industry]*

also meant that rail transport was becoming increasingly unsuitable for many classes of goods...The process of acquisition of long distance hauliers by the... Commission...was protracted and the impact on traffic flows as a result of the Commission's permit control was not noticeable before denationalisation was effected by the Transport Act 1953...[there was a 49% increase in public haulage vehicles between 1952 and 1968]. Whilst these were the golden years for road haulage they were black pages in railway history for not only were the number of road vehicles growing but also their size and carrying capacity... Despite its inherent weakness the licensing system did affect a degree of protection for the railways and did much to preserve for them the traffic which they were best fitted to carry. Whatever its failings the system produced order out of chaos in the 30s and provided a stable framework in the 50s on which the industry could reorganise in the inevitable confusion arising from nationalisation and de-nationalisation within a span of 6 years.

Licensing was neither an exact science nor a legalistic procedure but rather a successful blending of common sense and constantly refreshed background knowledge of the transport needs and availability applied to the evidence in each case with the public interest as the paramount consideration.'

He concluded:

'The fundamental differences between "quantity" and "quality" licensing systems are becoming increasingly obvious...Some side effects are worthy of comment. Perhaps the most noticeable are that a Licensing Authority no longer knows who carries what to where and that with the absence of objectors and the increase in disciplinary cases procedure tends to be inquisitorial in character. The faint aura of benevolent paternalism which touched carriers' licensing now carries more than a trace of the strict Victorian father...'

12 Operator licensing

The end of 1971, 1972 and the beginning of 1973 must have seemed very quiet years for the Commissioners. During 1971 operators' licensing became fully implemented. 1972 and 1973 were the years of the Prices and Incomes Policy with most areas reporting that there had been few fares applications and the ones that had been made were not major. The West Midland Commissioner was clearly scratching round for something to say, and politely he did not say that one company had come up with what he thought was a daft idea of:

> *'...season tickets in the form of a medallion worn around the neck for the benefit of congenitally disabled persons who from birth have suffered a serious arm deformity and cannot conveniently handle cash...Only one ticket has so far been sold...'*

The general impression given in the reports was that the Commissioners were supportive of the system of quality licensing for goods vehicles. One was not and in his report for 1973/4 the Commissioner for the Northern Traffic Area delivered a polemic (he was to retire in December 1975):

> *'With over 50 years in the service of the Crown and 21 years as Chairman of Traffic Commissioners in this Traffic Area, it would be a failure of duty if I did not report fully on my findings in the result of the changes in the licensing of heavy goods vehicles.*
>
> *The high rate of entry to and exit from the industry indicates that saturation point of operators and vehicles is long past. Every newcomer today is calculated to take work from an existing operator.*
>
> *Healthy competition has given way to wasteful competition of the worst kind.*

Excessive hours by drivers are extremely difficult to detect and even more difficult to prove in court.

The speed limit of 40 miles per hour for lorries on single and dual roads is flaunted from one end of the country to the other and gives grave concern both as to fuel consumption and road safety...Hauliers generally would obviously be reluctant to encourage tightening up in strict enforcement of speed limits since new vehicles are now plated...with substantial weight advantage to those with engine capacities giving speeds of 70 miles per hour and upwards.

A marked increase in the number of existing operators who have reduced the number of authorised...vehicles is a further indication that excessive numbers of goods vehicles are being licensed. This can be seen every day on any main road in the high proportion...travelling empty and in most cases, aggravating the excessive speeds...

Complaints are nation wide among professional hauliers of thefts of very expensive equipment and tackle such as tarpaulins, ropes, chains, spare wheels etc and even trailers.

Serious crimes are widespread against property in which heavy goods vehicles, of necessity, are used. This is not surprising since entry into this industry is not closed to shop breakers, thieves, receivers, and other active criminals known to the Police.

As in previous years the numbers of objections to applications are negligible under the present licensing system and the high standards of professionalism essential in such a vital industry are disappearing in the flood of newcomers and amateurs...'

The Eastern Commissioner was defensive of the system:

'I have noted that concern has been expressed in the industry that under existing legislation licences are obtained too easily by newcomers...Nevertheless one in three new applications failed to get a clear grant...after-grant inspections of operators' premises showed that a high proportion of new operators were maintaining satisfactory standards...'

After a quiet period the Commissioners had a very busy twelve months. Fares applications were back on the agenda as the Western Commissioner noted (and I well remember):

'The inflationary climate has been responsible for an unusually large crop of applications for increases in fares with, additionally those which had been frozen during the previous year (because of the Prices and Incomes Policy)... In the case of the subsidiaries of the NBC the introduction of a Pensions and

Death Benefit Scheme for hourly and weekly paid employees was a significant factor...'

The position was similar in other traffic areas as the Yorkshire Commissioners noted:

'During the year 20 days were occupied in considering general fares applications at Public Sittings. Each of the NBC subsidiary companies ... applied for increases twice during the year...At one sitting the Commissioners were invited to refuse the application on the grounds that all public transport should be free...'

The Commissioners had also had to deal with a major administrative matter:

'The oil shortage following disputes and unrest in the Middle East led to the Government decision to prepare for the introduction of fuel rationing. This involved a tremendous amount of extra work for the staff of the Traffic Area Office. Fuel coupons were issued to all holders of road service licences to cover their operations for the initial six months...'

The Metropolitan Commissioner also reminded everyone what a difficult time they had had but how well they had done:

'...notwithstanding additional burdens last winter arising out of the issue of fuel coupons during a period when office lighting and heating were severely curtailed...'

But on the bus side it had been very much business as usual:

'After a hearing lasting 7 days, we refused applications by Evan Evans Tours Ltd for 5 week-end express services between London and a number of University cities for the benefit of university students only...'

The mid-1970s was a quiet period on the goods side. The Commissioners had been trying to drum up business by encouraging local authorities to object to applications for operators' licences on the new ground given by the Road Traffic Act 1974. The Yorkshire Commissioner was very disheartened by the response as he said in the 1974/5 report:

'The hope was expressed in last years' report that local authorities would avail themselves of the opportunity given by the Road Traffic Act 1974...to object on the grounds of the unsuitability of operating centres...This expectation has not been realised...There has been no objection from any source...'

Until subsequent amendments to the law, this was never a very productive source of work for the Commissioners because in the next year the Transport

Tribunal decided that environmental issues were not relevant in deciding suitability.[80]

The Northern Commissioner became very upset with the Department of Transport, as he made abundantly clear:

> *'A serious delay in the actual issue of written authorisation for the movement of a winch for an important export order...had to be overcome by my personal intervention and that of a Deputy Secretary in your Department and an Assistant Chief Constable of Northumbria. The width of the load in question was found to be 7 inches over the free limit, it had to travel only a mile and a half to the Newcastle quay side and was held up for three days blocking in two other winches of the exact width inside the works of the manufacturers.*
>
> *Once the route in such cases is approved, authority should be delegated to the LA to issue the actual forms, instead of awaiting the signature of one very junior officer in London to be sent by post to remote parts of Great Britain...'*

On the 8 July 1975 he appointed Dr L C L (Leo) Blair as a Deputy Traffic Commissioner and Deputy Licensing Authority. He resigned from these two positions on 31 July 1977, but received no acknowledgement in the annual report.

Fortunately for the Commissioners the other side of their business was flourishing. The position as reported by the Yorkshire Commissioners was typical:

> *'Continuing and rising inflation has necessarily meant more applications for fares increases during the year. All six NBC subsidiaries...in this area found it necessary to make two applications for increases...The Commissioners declined to authorise automatic increases, but agreed a procedure whereby, on the occurrence of a "trigger", the application could be renewed without further publication...In the 1975 round similar supplementary applications were made, the "triggers" being successive increases of 2% of the basic annual operating costs shown in the main application...As we observed in last year's report, there is very little scope for successful objections to applications for fares increases which are kept within the limits of the Price Code...'*

A system of quality licensing for public service vehicle operators was still some years off, though the need for it was amply illustrated by a report from the same Commissioner:

> *'A PSV conveying 17 work girls to a mill was examined at the roadside and found to have an open gas fire bolted to the front bulkhead. On being questioned about this the driver walked to the rear of the coach and opened the*

boot where he turned a tap on a Calor gas bottle, then walked to the front, struck a match and lit the fire. This was a temporary heating system...'

Things were rather more up to date in the North-Western Traffic Area where Charles Hodgson presented his last report:

'An electric midi bus was certified in this Area...The Silent Rider electric bus described in last year's report continued in service...Development is now proceeding on an electric Public Service Vehicle where the batteries are transported in an attached trailer towed behind the vehicle...It may prove unsuitable for general service...'

His doubts seem to have been vindicated.

The reports for 1976/7 reflect the continuing large number of public sittings allotted to fares applications. The South Eastern Commissioner reported:

'The Commissioners sat for...nearly six working weeks during the year, hearing applications by NBC and municipal operators for variations of fares conditions. All the NBC subsidiaries operating in the Traffic Area had two applications heard during the year, with the exception of Southern Vectis who had only one; the Brighton Area Transport Services, operated in consortium by South Down Motor Services Ltd and Brighton Corporation were before the Commissioners three times...The Commissioners...feel that they have a minimal amount of room for manoeuvre, and can in practice interfere only where increases on individual fares appear 'unreasonable' in relation to the general level of increases. These occasions are very rare, if only because fares applications are prepared by the companies with great care...The Commissioners feel that they owe it to themselves to point out that on the three occasions in recent years when they ordered a significant reduction in the increase proposed...Your predecessor in office allowed the operators' appeals and restored the fares originally proposed...'

To some extent the South Eastern Commissioners had made a rod for their own backs because they required applicants to submit seventeen different schedules to support their applications, whilst in most other areas perhaps five or six were required. Lengthy public sittings were not limited to fares applications. The East Midland Commissioners had one long sitting:

'A public sitting lasting 15 days was held at Oxford to consider a number of applications for new and revised services submitted by City of Oxford Motor Services Limited, Worth Motor Services Limited and Carterton Coaches Limited...'

Whilst the Metropolitan Commissioner reported another long hearing:

> *'The hearing of applications by Wallace Arnold Tours Limited for 5 new express services from London via Dover to Moscow, Vienna, Barcelona, Athens and Istanbul occupied 11 days spread over the months of November 1976 to February 1977...'*

By 31 March 1977 no decision had been given.

13 Professional competence

The Commissioners were not short of work and whilst because of Cash & McCall they did not get the extra volume of work they expected, in the 1975/6 Report the Yorkshire Commissioner commented on the next wave of work about to hit them. Holders of standard operators' licences were going to be required to be or to employ a person who was professionally competent. Those with specified existing experience were going to be entitled as of right:

> *'Towards the end of the year our staff were becoming increasingly involved in the impending change in the pattern of licensing...The main involvement was to take the necessary steps to set up a register of persons who will be eligible for "Grandfather Rights"...As "professionally competent" in the context of "Standard" operators licences...and some 11,000 "invitations" were dispatched...'*

By the end of April 1978 that traffic area alone had issued 20,000 certificates. Some operators recognising the value of one of those small pieces of green paper were a little greedy as the Eastern Commissioner commented in 1977/8:

> *'In general, large operators nominated comparatively few employees, while some small partnerships tended to nominate the whole family. The ages of nominees ranged from 8 years to 89. In some applications there were many claimants in respect of few vehicles, the highest being 31 for one goods vehicle...'*

Throughout this period the Commissioners continued to deal with heavy goods vehicle licences and occasionally commented on the outcome of appeals to Magistrates' Courts against their refusal of a licence as did the Northern Commissioner in 1977/8 and 1978/9:

'The only appeal to the Magistrates Court came from a deaf and dumb driver whose application for a provisional licence had been refused because of his inability to communicate...the Magistrates dismissed the appeal...'

'There was one appeal to the Magistrates' Court...by a deaf person. This appeal was dismissed...'

The Report for 1977/8 covered Silver Jubilee Year. The Yorkshire Commissioner noted one major event that must have put considerable strain on the local transport system:

'As part of the Silver Jubilee celebrations a special event was held on 13 July at the Elland Road Football Ground in Leeds when the Queen was present. 40,000 school children had to be transported, on a very tight schedule to and from the ground...involving the use of 442 buses and 15 special trains...'

The North-Western Commissioner noted the difficulty in obtaining shorthand writers. By this time the Metropolitan Traffic Area had been using tape-recording for some time but now the North- Western Area had to follow suit. The shorthand writers were very much part of the scene of the public sittings. Many had covered the same traffic areas for years and some were real characters. One who normally covered the Western Area, ensconced on his blow-up rubber cushion, virtually dictated the length of a day's sitting, advised applicants, objectors, advocates and from time to time the Commissioners, before bouncing home in his Citroen Ami 6.

Fares applications remained a major issue with some Traffic Areas making life very difficult for operators. In the South Eastern Traffic Area the Commissioners reduced the major applications from the 17% gross sought to 11% and one Municipal had its application reduced by 50% to a 12.5% gross increase.

The powers of the Commissioners were further diluted by the Transport Act 1978. County Councils were required to produce five-year public transport plans which the Commissioners were required to take into account when dealing with road service licences.[81]

The 1978/9 Report highlighted what was in effect a national strike by lorry drivers. The last national strike in the bus industry had been relatively short and back in August 1957. The North Western Commissioner in particular commented on it though he seems to have been more interested in the impact on his staff than the nation as a whole:

'This year saw the disruption of the Road Haulage industry by the strikes of drivers at the end of 1978 and the beginning of 1979. These created a very considerable amount of extra work of an unusual nature for the staff of this Traffic Area Office requiring them to work long hours during the week, at week-ends and over public holidays at Christmas and New Year...'

The Eastern Commissioner seems to indicate that the rather secretive Regional Emergency Planning Committee (see page 39) might have been preparing to become involved:

> *'I must...express my special gratitude for the very great help given by members of the Regional Transport Sub-Committee and their organisations during the road haulage dispute in January and February 1979 and by the Traffic Area staff...who were co-opted...to staff the emergency room round-the-clock while the disputed lasted...'*

On the bus side, without recasting the basic legislation, the Road Traffic Act 1978 generally amended road service licensing criteria, giving greater emphasis to the needs of the public and in particular the disabled as well as recasting references to the public transport requirements of the area. These amendments gave a short-term boost to new applications and variations of existing licences.

The South Wales Commissioner noted a perennial complaint made to him, and one which has since been repeated frequently:

> *'...complaints are received that school contracts buses are overcrowded, but although all these complaints are investigated, no instance of overcrowding has been found. It is thought that the activities of exuberant schoolchildren give an impression of overcrowding!...'*

14 Jurisdiction removed

The Transport Act 1980 removed a substantial proportion of the Commissioners' jurisdiction. First it removed from express operations, and excursions and tours the requirement for a road service licence.[82] Second it empowered the Minister to designate 'trial areas'[83] where road service licences were not required for stage carriages.[84] Third it removed the general power to impose fares conditions.[85] Now they could only do so where it was essential 'to protect the public from unreasonable conduct by the holder of the licence' or to regulate terms of competition.[86] An operator could require the removal of fares conditions unless section 7(3) applied.[87] Fifth, they were given very limited powers to refuse a road service licence for routes which were not otherwise served.[88] They even lost a small element of their work by the abolition of the licensing of conductors.[89] That historically, in each year, many days of public sittings had been committed to exactly the kind of applications which now no longer would be made, gives some indication of the loss of work for the Commissioners.

That loss was to some extent alleviated by two other provisions of the Act. Section 5 now required them to grant road service licences, effectively for stage carriages, unless it was against the interests of the public. That was, on the face of it, likely to increase the number of such applications by encouraging existing operators and new comers. A more major and enduring accretion to their powers was the introduction of public service vehicle operators' licensing, generally mirroring goods vehicle operators' licences. The principal differences being that there were no provisions as to operating centres and individual licence discs were not required, the operator being issued with ones which could be transferred without formality between vehicles.[90] The disciplinary powers of revocation, suspension, curtailment and variation of conditions followed those of the goods regimen.[91] If 1980 ended with the Commissioners complaining of a headache it would not be surprising as they had also to deal with some 21 other sets of new or amending regulations.

The impending Act had not saved the Commissioners from large numbers of applications during the second part of 1979 and the first part of 1980 as the Eastern Commissioner commented:

> *'Given the national wage settlements of the winter of 1978/9, the severity of that winter...the steep increase in fuel costs, the general increase in the costs of goods and services bought in and the constraints on grant aid from local authorities it is hardly surprising that the year was notable for the number of applications for fares increases. All but one of the operators in the public sector sought and were granted two increases during the year; and the number of applications from independent operators more than doubled – from 247... to 546 in 1979/80...'*

Perhaps however the weather gave added verisimilitude to an event noted by the South Wales Commissioner:

> *'SANTA'S SPECIALS. On each of the three Saturdays before Christmas, Cardiff City Transport Department ran Santa Specials for children. There was a tour of the City in a decorated bus with music being played. Santa Claus was aboard to talk to the children and each child received a small gift of chocolate...'*

The Report of 1980/81 shows that the Commissioners were still capable of being 'miffed' by decisions of the Magistrates. Perhaps they felt that lay magistrates over-ruling them on their special areas of jurisdiction and expertise affected the respect due to their office. Nevertheless one can sympathise with the Yorkshire Commissioner:

> *'One of the decisions [of magistrates on an appeal against the refusal of an HGV licence on medical grounds] was especially surprising since it appeared to mitigate (sic) against the recommendation of the Medical Advisory Branch of the Department, advocating the policy of the Medical Council on Accident Prevention, and it was even more surprising to find that the applicant was awarded £300 costs against the Department...'*

Whether they realised it or not at the time sections 1 and 7 Transport Act 1980 together with section 33 of the 1981 Act sounded the death knell of road service licensing. The Bus Services in Trial Areas Regulations 1981 effectively deregulated buses in the designated areas. The volume of work available to the Traffic Commissioners was beginning to wane. The Western Commissioner commented:

> *'We have now had a full year free from the burden of hearing applications for fares revisions. The long drawn out public sittings held in the past had ceased to be of any real value and we have had no evidence that operators have made unreasonable use of their freedom...'*

No doubt Parliament had intended that the shifting of the burden of proof to the objectors would open up the market to a greater degree of competition. That was not always what happened. There were few who were prepared to take on the major operators (unless they were major operators themselves). The potential objectors were prepared to stand their ground and fight it out. But the attempts to take advantage of the 1980 Act certainly kept the Commissioners in the market of holding public sittings, though as it turned out it was their swan song. The Western Commissioner commented on both aspects:

'...there have been very few applications from existing operators to extend their ordinary stage service operations or from new applicants to enter this field. This lack of applications has not come as any great surprise. In many cases it requires a real sense of dedication to become involved in the hazardous business of such operation...the first challenge to a network of these services provided by an NBC subsidiary was an application by a well known independent operator – Swanbrook Transport – for a comprehensive service of stage carriage in the north west part of Bristol...by the end of the year the Public Sitting had taken up 5 days spread over some 10 weeks and, on present form, it seems likely that a further 3 or 4 days will be required...'

We need to go to his next year's report to get to the end of that story and to see the fate of another who challenged an NBC subsidiary and a municipal in the same application:

'The Public Sitting held for the Swanbrook Transport applications for a comprehensive service of stage carriages in the north west part of the Bristol City operating area...was completed on 4 May after taking up some 9 days spread over some 3½ months.

That application was followed later in the year by further applications by 2 small Devon operators, one for 2 stage services in Exeter and the other for 2 stage services in Plymouth. The 2 stage services applied for in Exeter would, for the most part, have operated in direct competition with the closely integrated net work of stage services provided by the Western National Omnibus Company Limited...in Exeter and much the same position would have applied to the 2 stage services in Plymouth where the integrated network of services was provided by Plymouth City Transport and Western National. Not surprisingly the two NBC subsidiaries, Plymouth City Transport and Devon County Council, strongly objected to the four applications. The Exeter Public Sitting occupied some four days spread over some two months and the Plymouth...took up six days, also spread over some 2 months.

In the light of all the evidence...we were satisfied that the disadvantages to the public resulting from the loss of revenue if the applications were granted

> *outweighed the advantages to be gained to such an extent that there would be significant damage to the public interest...We therefore refused all the applications...'*

I well remember these cases as the advocate for the objectors. A huge effort was put into opposing the applications by both the operators and the county councils who saw potential success as being the 'thin end of the wedge'. It is interesting to note that after deregulation Swanbrook did not revive its interest in Bristol and no other applications of any real significance occurred in the area.

Applicants in other traffic areas were more successful. The South Eastern Commissioners commented on an application in Reading, which was the first of a number of new battles between the NBC and Reading Corporation:

> *'An application which tested the provisions of the Transport Act 1980 and illustrated the switch of the burden of proof from applicants to objectors was that made by Thames Valley and Aldershot Motor Services Limited to provide a new service from Reading Town Centre to a new supermarket outside the Borough boundary. The application was objected to by the Police, Reading Borough Transport and Berkshire County Council...*
>
> *The Police objection related to a road junction...a case had not been made out...on those grounds.*
>
> *...Reading...Transport objected primarily on the grounds of abstraction of traffic. They did not however...discharge the onus of proving that a grant would be against the public interest...*
>
> *...Berkshire County Council objected...as being against their published policy of discouraging competition with Reading...Transport in the area of Greater Reading. The Commissioners were not persuaded that the existence of such policy of itself was decisive of the issue, and were not satisfied on the rest of the evidence that a grant would be against the public interest...'*

15 The Transport Act 1982

By the time for the 1981/2 Report the implementation of the Transport Act 1982 was looming. The Commissioners had seemed supportive of the requirement that operating centres for goods vehicles should be 'suitable' and disappointed by the Cash & McCall decision removing environmental considerations from the equation. It should have followed that they would have been supportive of the Transport Act 1982 requiring operating centres to be suitable on environmental grounds.[92] Apart from any other factor, it was likely to give them added work which in the past they seemed generally to have welcomed and also, as it turned out, was to be useful in replacing some of the work lost when buses were deregulated under the Transport Act 1985. The West Midland Commissioner was particularly concerned, but got in an early plea for additional staff:

> *'I await the implementation of the Transport Act 1982 with some apprehension. I have not yet seen the complicated regulations which are being drafted... I regret that you were not able to accept my advice that these matters could very simply and more appropriately be dealt with by local planning authorities who are statutorily responsible for environmental matters. A simple procedure could have been evolved. As it is, there is no doubt I shall require more staff to deal with all the objections and representations which are bound to result from the local advertisement of applications for operator licences...'*

The same report contains an apparent non-sequitur which still puzzles me:

> *'Two of the dynamic weighbridge sites in the Warwickshire area were out of use for two months, whilst preparation was made for and during the Pope's visit...'*

Was it because he feared that some Protestants might try to weigh the Pope-mobile and find it overweight? I suppose we shall never know.

One is always led to believe that the Swiss are a particularly law abiding nation. It seems not always so as the Eastern Commissioner reported in the same year:

'Proceedings were taken against two Swiss drivers for overloading offences. Both drivers had been checked and their vehicles had been found to be overloaded. After off-loading the excess weights the drivers waited until the examiners had left, then put the excess weight back on the vehicles and continued their journeys. These two drivers returned to the country about 10 days later. They were taken to court immediately...each driver was fined £300...'

The 1982/3 Report shows that the 1982 Act was having mixed effects across the country. The North-Western Commissioner reported that attempts by new operators to "cream off" profitable services had been few and far between. The exceptions were in the East Midland Traffic Area:

'In Nottingham, Leicester and Lincoln however operators have been in exceptionally active competition for routes and services. Competition between the main operators in Leicester has led to some friction...'

As I remember the cases in Leicester that is slight understatement of the relations between Midland Fox and Leicester City Transport as they fought over 'area stop signs' and services to the estates surrounding the City.

What, to a non-nuclear-scientist, seems to have been a potentially more explosive situation arose in the South Eastern area:

'An interesting problem that arose...was the landing of a vehicle loaded with cylinders containing solid uranium hexafluoride, 1880 kilograms in excess of permissible weight limit and with no international road permit for the journey, resulting in the Department advising the French Ministry of Transport that this type of vehicle would not be allowed into the United Kingdom...'

The new environmental provisions were due to come into effect on 1 June 1984. During 1983 a consultation exercise was carried out and the Northern Commissioner noted that there was considerable depth of feeling in the trade about the changes though he thought that many of the fears were exaggerated.

On the 1 April 1984 the Northern and the Yorkshire and East Midland Traffic Areas ceased to exist. Yorkshire and part of the Northern was absorbed into a new North Eastern Area, the remainder of the Northern into the North Western Area whilst the East Midland was shared between the West Midlands and the Eastern. The West Midlands also noted the appointment of one John Pugh as a Deputy Licensing Authority.

Road service licensing was not quite dead but certainly in its death throes. Midland Fox and Leicester City Transport were still fighting it out, as Ken Peter made clear in his last report before retirement:

'At a 2 day Public Sitting at Leicester the Commissioners considered, with much media attention, 6 applications for new services together with 3 applications to vary existing services made by Midland Fox Limited against a background of competition and objections from Leicester City Transport. The applications were for high frequency minibus services into areas not conveniently served by larger vehicles and extending the range of connecting services. The Commissioners granted these applications with conditions restricting the number of vehicles permitted to use certain bus stops in any one hour...'

Matters even began to liven up on the Isle of Wight as the South Eastern Commissioner noted, a portent of things to come:

'Four...days...were devoted to one case. This arose from a package of applications submitted by the Southern Vectis Omnibus Company Limited for revision of services in the Isle of Wight which attracted objections from local residents. The first day of the sitting was held at Cowes and a further three days were spent at Newport. The applications were eventually granted as applied for...'

The break-up of The National Bus Company had been foreshadowed by section 1 Transport Act 1982 but it was section 47 of the Transport Act 1985 that imposed the requirement of a scheme for the transfer of the Company to the private sector. The impact of that on the Commissioners concerned was slight. The major impact of the Act came from section 1 which abolished road service licensing and substituted a system of registration for local services (in essence the old stage carriage services). Thus a system introduced in 1930 came to an end. Section 3 provided 'There shall cease to be a body of traffic commissioners.' But the Chairmen themselves were saved. Section 4 provided that there should be a Traffic Commissioner for each traffic area who was to hold office during Her Majesty's pleasure with a requirement to retire before becoming 66. The Minister also relieved himself of the burden of dealing with appeals from the Commissioners by assigning them to the Transport Tribunal.[93] Public sittings now became public inquiries.[94]

The Commissioners' other powers were not in general recast. They continued with their powers in relation to PSV operators' licences and were given supervisory and punitive powers in relation to registered local services. Operators who failed to operate a local service or operated one in contravention of the Act could lose the right to operate a particular registered service or local services generally. Those who intentionally interfered with the operations of another operator, or operated a local service in a manner dangerous to the public would similarly face the ire of the Commissioner.[95]

They had some warning of the problems they might face in disciplining bus companies before the Act. In his 1983/4 report the Eastern Commissioner reported:

> *'Complaints were made to us that a rural service was not being operated to timetable...We held a public sitting which was attended by a large number of users...We found that the weight of opinion was strongly in favour of the licence-holder continuing to operate the service, even if it was not always run according to the timetable – it being better to have some service rather than none.*
>
> *This was the first case within memory when we have had to consider whether to revoke or suspend a road service licence for contravention of a condition...It illustrates the practical difficulties of taking effective action...'*

These powers were needed and became more frequently used over the years. The deregulation under the Act did not quite take bus operations back to 1929 though in some areas one might have been forgiven for thinking all control of local services had been abandoned as the newly privatised ex-NBC companies came into conflict with one another, with the municipals and with entirely new operators. For the observer it was great fun; for the Commissioners often a headache; for the travelling public often disbelief.

Traffic area boundaries

1985

1993

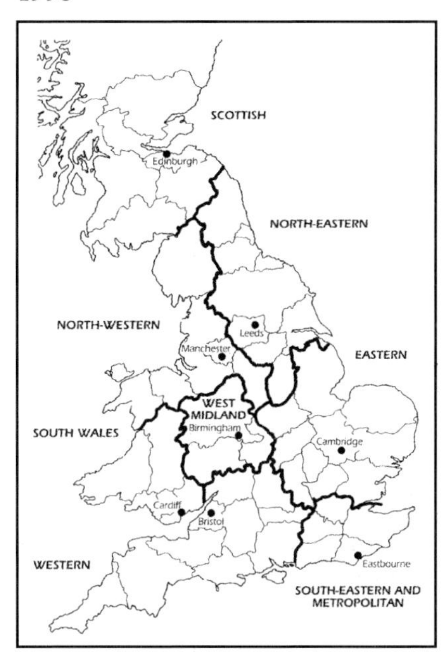

2005

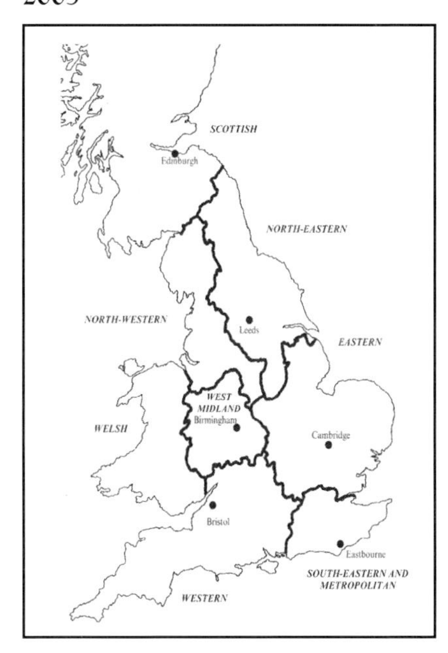

16 Environmental impact

Environmental provisions were beginning to have a real impact on the Commissioners by the time of the 1985/6 Reports leading not only to a considerable increase in the office work but also the number of actual or potential public inquiries. In his last Report before retirement after nine years in office one Commissioner commented:

> *'Members of the public – even those who have come into contact with more than one application which affects them – and have been to more than one public inquiry – seemingly have not, cannot and probably will not fully understand the complexities of the legislation...Hopes are raised then all too frequently dashed...they feel the die is loaded in favour of the operator...'*

The South Eastern Commissioner in his last report after 10 years in office pointed out that it was not only the public who got it wrong:

> *'...some authorities still advance arguments on "pure" planning grounds and may be represented at public inquires by Planning Officers who are unable to deal with points of law affecting the relevance or admissibility of their evidence and arguments...'*

It might not be unfair to point out that the Commissioners did not always get it right either as the Transport Tribunal pointed out from time to time.

No doubt the Commissioners had a sudden accretion in the volume of work from that source but also, on the bus side, operators had to register, by 28 February 1986, the commercially viable services which they wished to operate from 26 October after which there was effectively a freeze until 26 January 1987. Operators had approached registration in many different ways but it was clear that many had not got it right. That led to a scramble in 1987 to vary registrations or effect new ones. The North Eastern Commissioner was no doubt not the only one to notice these developments:

'...both my offices are still receiving large numbers of variation applications [of registrations] as operators continually assess the viability of their commercial services or strive to match timetable changes by their competitors – often on a tit-for-tat basis. This high level of competition has led...to certain operational malpractices including excessive duplication of services...'

And the South Eastern Commissioner was perhaps the first since the 1920s to use the phrase 'bus wars':

'I should just mention the much publicised "bus wars" that have arisen... It was inevitable that well established operators should resent intrusion into their territory...In one or two cases this competitiveness has given rise to practices that are certainly unfair and, in one or two cases, verge on dangerous... I do remain concerned about the City of Oxford, Southampton and the Isle of Wight...'

War of another sort was happening on buses and the Commissioners maintained their concern about it (and sympathy with the operators):

'Late night services on Saturdays and Sundays were withdrawn by Plymouth Citybus because of unacceptable levels of hooliganism and vandalism. In one instance a driver was hit on the head with a glass bottle whilst going to the assistance of a passenger who was being threatened. There were many instances of windows being pushed out and seats being slashed. At one stage police were riding "shot-gun"...There was one serious knife attack on a Wilts and Dorset...driver which resulted in a 6 month prison sentence for the attacker... There were 13 assaults on drivers on Bristol Omnibus services...'

By the time of their 1987/9 Reports the Commissioners were well into trying to deal with 'bus wars'. The North East was one of the areas much affected:

'The competition...is so intense that some towns and cities are saturated with buses...Certain large operators seem determined not to allow smaller operators to gain a foothold...and...sometimes register high frequency services identical to the small operator with the result that the small operator finds it impossible to run either according to timetable – because of vehicle saturation at bus stops and bus stations – or economically...'

Problems were not restricted to the north because the Eastern Commissioner was also reporting:

'Without doubt, the current legislation has generated more competition between operators, occasionally to the point where blows have been exchanged or vehicles damaged...It is...my experience that when an operator is concerned about the operations of others, he expects his allegations to be accepted as firm evidence which is sufficient to warrant severe action on my part...when

allegations are made against him, he expects his denials or excuses to be accepted without question...'

The Commissioners were struggling to find the most suitable and effective remedy. The most obvious was section 111 which could result in the operator being required to refund an amount equivalent to 20 per cent of the fuel tax rebate entitlement for the previous three months. This could be a six-figure sum for some of the large operators. This was an all or nothing approach and the sum was often potentially disproportionate. The Commissioners suggested that it was too blunt an instrument and that the section should be amended to allow for proportionality. It was some years before that happened. Faced with these problems maybe Ronald Jackson was pleased to retire, though he remained on as a Deputy Traffic Commissioner for two areas until suffering a fatal heart attack in the West Midland Traffic Office on 28 July 1988.

In the past Commissioners had commented on severe winter weather conditions. There was a more sinister twist to the weather report from the North-Western Commissioner in 1988/9:

'The mild weather resulted in an exceptionally good year for enforcement...'

There was obvious concern about two reports that were in the course of preparation. There was the Arman Review of Operators Licensing and the Palmer Review of Traffic Area Offices. With nothing to risk as a retiring Traffic Commissioner the Scottish Commissioner urged the Minister:

'I ask you to give due weight to the advantages of a statutory independent organisation locally based and sensitive to local differences of economics, geography and culture. The alternative of deciding matters at the centre, with full Ministerial responsibility and accountability for decisions, is not one which attracts me nor, I am certain, the road transport industry as a whole...'

Perhaps the only good news of the year was the move of the Metropolitan Area Office from the depressingly gloomy (prison hospital?) at Bromyard Avenue, Acton to smart High Street, Kensington.

Despite their fears little came of the Palmer Report other than the appointment of a Senior Traffic Commissioner, who was not necessarily the senior in post and with no additional legal powers.

1991 was not a good year for the Commissioners. The Metropolitan Traffic Area ceased to exist on 1 June 1991 and on 1 April they had lost vocational licensing to the DVLA [Driver and Vehicle Licensing Agency] and traffic examiners to the Vehicles Inspectorate Agency [VI]. Most of the Metropolitan Traffic Area was transferred to the newly named South Eastern and Metropolitan Traffic Area based in the delightfully named but mundane office block, at Ivy House, Ivy Terrace, Eastbourne. It was also the year in which the South Wales Commissioner was way too optimistic when he reported:

> *'Now that the future of the Cardiff office has been finally resolved I and the staff can look forward to continue to serve the Industry without the fear of further cutbacks or even closure...a nod of appreciation to those in Marsham Street [London home of the Department for Transport] who made the future of Cardiff office certain...'*

Perhaps the most significant feature of 1993/4 was that for the first time North-Western [as in North-Western Traffic Area] appeared without a hyphen.

Occasionally Commissioners made statements which lawyers stored away as forming part of an appeal should it become necessary. In his 1994/5 report the North Western Commissioner went a little further than was perhaps wise:

> *'Operators who appear at disciplinary inquiries must expect action against their licences...'*

The West Midland Commissioner put it a little more circumspectly:

> *'...the Licensing Review Board...only refer cases to Public Inquiry where there is a high probability of disciplinary action being taken against the licence...'*

The bus and lorry operators were now, in the jargon of the day, becoming 'customers' though they had no choice of supplier:

> *'Great emphasis is place on the customer care aspect of our work and I am sure that the efforts made by staff to implement the changes to the legislation will contribute greatly to the provision of a helpful and friendly service to operators...'*

This fits uncomfortably with what seems to have been a concerted approach to the issue of enforcement (and possibly a response to the re-organisation which created the Vehicle Inspectorate Agency under Area Managers). The Eastern Commissioner led the attack in his Goods Vehicle report:

> *'Once Parliament had decided to abandon the quantity control of goods vehicles in favour of a stricter regime of quality control – recognised by the 1968 Act – it was axiomatic that effective enforcement would be the price that had to be paid for this liberal approach. Thus the need for this enforcement now lies at the very heart of the licensing system: without it not only is road safety jeopardised, but the law-abiding operator becomes disenchanted with a regime that seems to allow cheats to prosper. In sum the system loses its credibility... the over all results seem to indicate that the VI in my area are either targeting badly or simply failing to prosecute...'*

This was followed up on the bus side in the North Eastern Report:

> *'I am surprised that, while there has been a 29% increase in the number of vehicles checked by Traffic Examiners and a 48% increase in the number of tachographs screened, the number of prosecutions has fallen by 13% and the number of drivers' hours offences has fallen by 20%. I shall look to VI to improve on their success rate in this area of their work next year...'*

The next year saw the Eastern Commissioner repeating the theme:

> *'...one must question either the effectiveness of the targeting or the will to prosecute ...'*

and in the 1994/5 report the Metropolitan Commissioner began to see dangers:

> *'... the Inspectorate has a revised target for next year. It is to weigh 25% less vehicles but maintain prosecutions and prohibitions at their current level. The incentive will surely be to prohibit and prosecute at lower levels. The revised target is questionable...We need to get the rogue operator off the road. That should be the Vehicle Inspectorate's target, not meeting a set number of prosecutions or prohibitions...'*

This, whilst not the beginning, was certainly a point from which lawyers and the industry sensed that the Vehicle Inspectorate and to some extent the Commissioners were under the pressure of targets.

17 Continuous licensing

The Goods Vehicles (Licensing of Operators) Act 1995 was a useful consolidation with some significant amendments. The title of 'licensing authority', used since the 1968 Act when dealing with goods vehicle licensing, disappeared and Traffic Commissioner was to be used for both goods vehicle and public passenger vehicle functions.[96] 1 January 1996 saw the introduction of continuous licensing for goods vehicles with a 'review' of road safety and environmental matters every five years.[97] Unless an operator applied for a variation or a new licence there would be no more advertising of the existence of an operating centre and no automatic five year reminder to operators of the risks of losing it or having conditions imposed. The West Midland Commissioner gave a timely reminder of the basis of 'O' licensing in the 1995/6 Report:

> *'Operators must realise, that with the advent of indefinite licensing, the operator licensing system depends even more on truth and trust and those who fail to comply with their statements of intent can expect to be seriously disciplined...'*

Concerned as ever by their fluctuating workload, and no doubt by the implications of such reduction, the Metropolitan Commissioner commented:

> *'Dispensing with renewals and the need for advertising and publication has reduced the bureaucratic burden on operators. It is also reducing significantly the workload in my office. The Review procedure which was in effect introduced to compensate for the demise of the renewal application and, in particular, to safeguard the rights of Local Authorities and local residents to complain about operating centres, is not producing the level of representations expected (in fact 1 in 500 rather then 15 in 500). 'The benefit to operators is obvious but local residents are unlikely to be pleased...'*

January 1997 saw the unpopular move of the North Western Area office to Leeds and in March the equally unpopular one of the South Wales office to Birmingham.

In his 1996/7 Report the Eastern Commissioner set out what seemed to be a 'mission statement' for goods vehicle 'O' licensing:

> *'It is not difficult to get an operator's licence. There are few hurdles to climb and those that do exist are set fairly low...But that is the intention I imagine: a system that does not discourage enterprising souls from having a go.*
>
> *The price to pay for such a liberal approach, however, is effective enforcement in order to weed out the operator who, in the light of his subsequent failure to fulfil the undertakings he made to get the licence, should not have been granted one in the first place. Proper enforcement, therefore, lies at the heart of the licensing system: without it not only is road safety jeopardised, but the law abiding operator becomes disenchanted with a regime that seems to allow cheats to prosper. In short, the system loses its credibility. It follows that one of my main preoccupations is to encourage the flow of information... thereafter to call the errant operator to a Public Inquiry, at which I can consider the use of the swingeing powers at my disposal...The information I require is held by a variety of agencies but its (sic)' often like getting blood out of a stone. When one considers that the first meeting of the Traffic Commissioners took place on 21 January 1931 – and the problem was recognised in those early days – it is disappointing that it continues to exist in 1997...'*

1997/8 saw the end of separate Reports for the goods and PSV licensing systems. Reports were becoming shorter and the individuality of each Commissioner less apparent. Perhaps to counter that fact, the 1998/9 Report was the first to contain photographs of the Commissioners and a more than ample demonstration of their ability to compose bar and pie charts on their computers. The year also saw the creation of a Welsh Traffic Area by the incorporation of north Wales from the North Western Traffic Area into the South Wales Traffic Area. Before that took effect the North Western Area heard the first Public Inquiry to be conducted in the Welsh language with simultaneous translation into English and Welsh.

The 1999/2000 Report recorded the first appointment of a woman as Traffic Commissioner. Mrs. Beverley Bell, a solicitor, was not only the first woman to be appointed but at 40 was also the youngest appointee. Until this stage the general impression had perhaps been that, with some exceptions, the appointment to Commissioner was not a primary career move, but often a recognition of past services in some other field. The selection of a 40 year old woman from a field of some 400 applicants will no doubt give a new dynamic to the perception of the Commissioners and the relationships between them. This new Commissioner set out her 'mission statement' in her first report:

> *'I am delighted that the North West once again has it's (sic) own Traffic Commissioner and I intend to raise the profile of the role of the Traffic Commissioner specifically within the North West Region...'*

The next year she took it one stage further in a campaign that was eventually successful in 2005:

> *'... as I travel around the North West I am asked when the North West Traffic Area Office will be re-opened... I have been struck by the strength of feeling in favour of a re-establishment of the Commissioner in the North West. I therefore feel that my aim for the future must be to respond to that feeling...'*

A similar feeling expressed in Wales the same year has not been satisfied:

> '...*she* [the Welsh Assembly member with responsibility for transport] *would like the Welsh Traffic Area to have an administrative presence in Wales; this remains a political matter...'*

During this period the Traffic Commissioners were calling many major bus operators before them for failing to operate local services in accordance with their timetables.[98] First they set an apparent standard of taking into account operations that were more than five minutes early or late, subsequently revised to one minute early and five minutes late on not more than 5 per cent of observed occasions. They used the swingeing power to 'fine' the companies the 20 per cent of the fuel rebate. This power was modified by the Transport Act 2000 so that the 'fine' could be up to £550 per vehicle authorised on the licence.[99] The amendment tended to increase the number of 'fines' though keeping them in five figures rather than six in the case of major operators. Commissioners were unsympathetic to the operators' explanations that time keeping was affected by traffic problems, particularly congestion. The Western Commissioner reported in 2000/1:

> *'Often bus operators claim, when faced with a failure to run a registered service in accordance with the particulars registered ... that traffic congestion provides them with a reasonable excuse and that they should not suffer a financial penalty as a result. Unless the traffic congestion is unanticipated, the operator should consider changing the registered particulars (i.e. the timetable) because it is the operator's timetable, not that of the Traffic Area Office...'*

At least the South Eastern and Metropolitan Commissioner acknowledged that it was not always the fault of the operators:

> '*In the light of this decision by one police force in my Area* [not to prosecute for breach of bus lane restrictions], *which I believe to be unfair both to the operator and to its passengers and which may not be unique, I propose to seek to persuade chief constables...that greater importance should be given to...bus lanes...*'

Many operators must have wondered whether the Commissioners appreciated the irony of their attitude towards timetabling when compared with their own problems and excuses in relation to the implementation of their computer system TAN 21. The 2001/2 Report indicated that they had a general concern about it. Whether it was to meet the requirement of the system or not, they compounded problems being suffered by operators by increasing from 42 days to 50 days the notice period for changing registration of local services.

In the 2002/3 Report Michael Betts, in his last year as Senior Commissioner, bewailed the position:

> '*The year under report has without doubt been the most difficult in my experience. I was sadly over-optimistic when I hoped last year, with regard to the introduction of the new TAN 21 computer system, that 'the promised land' was just over the horizon...it was found in practice that there were far more problems than had been anticipated. This in turn led to serious delays in processing applications and, along with problems associated with our new telephone system and inexperienced temporary staff, it resulted in many operators being faced with real difficulties for too long...*'

A paragraph or so later he said:

> '*...the Commissioners published a paper setting out what they saw as appropriate standards for local services' timekeeping...It has to be said that the industry has not been entirely happy with this...*'

It is true, it was not, but neither was it happy with the extension of 42 to 50 days, the delays in processing papers work, the problems with the telephones and the Commissioners' temporary staff, but they had no powers to 'fine' the Commissioners!

The Commissioners had other problems. They survived one challenge when the Transport Tribunal found that the statutory duties of the Commissioners did not contravene the Human Rights Act 1998.[100] They were also concerned at the loss of their Administrative Directors and later, in the 2001/2 Report, over what was effectively the merger of their staff with those of the Vehicle Inspectorate [VI]. The South Eastern and Metropolitan Commissioner wrote:

'The Traffic Commissioners were not consulted before the announcement was made, and they have expressed to the DfT their anxieties that the proposed merger... may prejudice the real and the perceived independence of a system that has been trusted by operators and their legal representatives for over 70 years...'

By the next year his concerns had not been addressed though the merger had taken place on 1 April 2003 (that date again) to form the Vehicle and Operator Services Agency (VOSA):

'Over 12 months later, I very much regret that answers have not been received from the Department for Transport to detailed questions put by the Traffic Commissioners to the Department.

Such a delay in responding to the anxieties expressed above seems inexplicable, and would be inexcusable from staff in my office...'

The Goods Vehicles (Enforcement Power) Regulations 2001 which gave powers to the Inspectorate to impound vehicles apparently not authorised under an 'O' licence was seen as a major step forward in enforcement. It also gave a boost to the work of the Commissioners because any appeal against the impounding went to them and it increased the number of applications for a licence as was noted by the North Eastern Commissioner in the 2002/3 Report:

'The effect of impounding has been dramatic. The number of previously unlicensed operators applying for licences...has increased markedly...'

He also noted that of 28 vehicles impounded 27 had been in a dangerous condition.

The North Western Commissioner took a 'busman's holiday':

'I escaped from the office for a two-week period to undertake my Certificate of Professional Competence (National Road Haulage Operations) examination in March 2002. I am delighted (and relieved) to report that I passed that examination...'

One imagines that few examinees have awaited the outcome of an examination with more trepidation.

The South Eastern and Metropolitan Commissioner was seen as championing the operator, as Commissioners have often done:

'If an operator, and particularly one with one vehicle or a small fleet, is unable to obtain a timely appointment for clearance [of a delayed prohibition notice] *at a test centre, a delayed prohibition notice can have the de facto effect of suspending or curtailing a licence without the safeguard of the independent Public Inquiry and the rights of appeal that gives...This cannot*

be right or fair, and I invite the VI to investigate the problem and address it, if necessary by more staff or longer hours ...'

It is for the reader to decide whether or not the collegiate photograph of all seven Commissioners in the 2004/5 Reports adds to confidence. One may reflect that there is not one knight, no Q.C., and no soldier above the rank of Brigadier. Some things have not changed others have reverted to an earlier practice. The Commissioners now meet together four times a year as they did back in the 1930s. There may be other changes down the line. The Senior Commissioner, referring to the Better Regulation Task Force, thought that by 2006 there might be a move to one traffic area for England.

Perhaps more worrying for the two industries is that at least two of the Commissioners have real concerns about the continuing independence of Traffic Commissioners. If they have concerns, so should the industries and all who appear before them. The trust I referred to at the beginning remains as essential now as it was back in 1931. Perhaps while the Commissioners are prepared to speak out as the West Midland Commissioner and particularly the South Eastern and Metropolitan Commissioner have done, we shall be able to celebrate 100 years of the Traffic Commissioners:

'The anxieties about independence...remain and have perhaps increased. It is not only imperative that the quasi-judicial position of the Traffic Commissioners when exercising their licensing and regulatory functions, and the preparation of papers by their staff, remain wholly and transparently independent of VOSA, but it is also important that VOSA recognises and accepts the independence of Traffic Commissioners and the staff working for them. I am becoming increasingly concerned that pressure may be put on staff serving Traffic Commissioners which may compromise the independence of Traffic Commissioners, especially when VOSA claims in its Business Plan, 2004-2005 that its responsibilities include 'operator licensing and bus registration services.'[101]

University of Salford transport collection

The CIT NW Section's library of transport texts was built up over 70 years by graduates and students donating books that they then shared When the library was displaced from Rail House, Manchester, where it had been latterly cared for by Jack Cryer MCIT, it found a temporary home at Manchester College of Arts and Technology.

However, when that college's connection with CIT courses ceased in 1993, the collection, together with additions made by the college librarian and retiring staff, was moved to the library of the University of Salford, where there are a number of undergraduate and postgraduate transport courses.

At the time, the university and Salford Technical College were in the process of a merger. This involved consolidating the two institutions' libraries at a single site. In this process, the stockpile comprising the NWCIT collection, containing many priceless and now out of print early texts, was mistaken for surplus book stock and disposed of.

The University of Salford librarian and the CILT GM branch recognise that this was a genuine though tragic error.

Accordingly, the librarian has made a generous offer to allow any members of CILT(UK) – not just North-West Region members – to make use of the university library, on production of their membership cards. There are, in fact, books in the library that duplicate quite a few of those lost, and, more importantly, there are many more valuable and up-to-date transport books.

The Greater Manchester Branch Chairman has received a letter from the Director of Information Services at Salford University confirming this agreement. The letter will be posted on the Branch's Web site: www.iltgm.org.uk

Meanwhile the Committee urges all members who would find this facility useful to avail themselves of it.

18 Final submission

My final submission, as lawyers are wont to say:

This personal view of the Commissioners over 75 years has looked primarily at what the Commissioners themselves have said. Throughout the period they have been supported by deputies, who seem generally not to have sought preferment; two did, John Mervyn Pugh and Philip Brown. The Commissioners gave routine thanks to their deputies in the conclusions to most of their Reports. It is perhaps worthwhile recording the special thanks to a busman who became one of the outstanding Deputy Commissioners, as a memorial to many:

> *'I commence my report by paying tribute to Brian Horner who has been a Deputy Traffic Commissioner for 15 years, during which time he had presided at 3000 Public Inquiries...Brian Horner was respected by transport trade organisations and operators alike and was well known for his unfailing courtesy...'*

In 1930 there were thirteen traffic areas and thirteen Chairmen of the Traffic Commissioners. Now there are eight areas and seven Traffic Commissioners two of whom are female (about the number of female bus drivers to be found in any traffic area in 1931). The now Senior Traffic Commissioner, Philip Brown noted in his 2002/3 Report that in one survey the traffic commissioners were described as 'struggling to throw off their 1930s persona', an unfair comment.

75 years on they have a very different role. They no longer control the quantity of buses and lorries on the road. In some ways they have a more difficult primary task, that of ensuring the quality of those operations. The task is one which they are only likely to achieve if they can carry the two huge industries with them. That seven individuals appear so to do speaks much of individual ability but also much for the trust and belief of those industries in their predecessors.

John Mervyn Pugh, who at one time or another was Traffic Commissioner for four traffic areas, in a recent conversation identified the cardinal point. The Commissioners have always been their own men. Appointed during Her Majesty's pleasure, they have been able to stamp their personalities on their traffic areas, and whilst occasionally they have upset operators and lawyers and we suspect, even secretly hope, the Department, their integrity and enthusiasm for the industries they have supervised has never been doubted.

Acknowledgements

All the errors and omissions (and I am sure there are many) are mine and mine alone. I have received particular help from Chris Heaps (Traffic Commissioner for the South Eastern and Metropolitan TA; Philip Brown the Senior Traffic Commissioner and Traffic Commissioner for the Western Area; Michael Betts (former Senior Traffic Commissioner); Joan Aitken Traffic Commissioner for the Scottish Area loaned some invaluable material from before the Second World War. Beverley Bell, Traffic Commissioner for the North Western Area gave insights from the distaff side. Brigadier Michael Turner, in particular, helped with his knowledge of the Regional Emergency Planning Committees. John Mervyn Pugh gave a wide overview and some unprintable anecdotes. I have admired the skills of David Lowe as editor without whom this document could not have been brought to publication. And my thanks are also extended to many others (including my wife who, by trying to correct this text, has learned more about what I did for 40-odd years than she ever knew at the time).

Geoffrey Jones
2006

Footnotes

Thomas Denner Corpe (Colonel T. D. Corpe O.B.E., T.D.) was admitted as a solicitor in April 1929 and became a partner in A. W. Taylor Son & Corpe. He was asked by the Bristol Tramways and Carriage Company Limited to read up the Transport Act 1930 and it was natural that he should follow that with the Road and Rail Traffic Act 1933. He soon became recognised as a specialist in those two fields of law. He served in the North Somerset Yeomanry during the war taking one of his clerks as his groom.

After war service he returned to the law and A. W. Taylor Son & Corpe merged with another old Bristol firm Danger & Cartwright, which traced its foundation to Mr. Thomas Danger who started practising in 1836, to form Cartwright Taylor & Corpe. He was back in practice in time for the nationalisation of the road haulage industry in 1947 and remained in practice until 1971. During this period he was the editor or co-editor of three editions of the standard reference book on road haulage licensing.

When I joined the firm on 27 December 1963 his other interest (apart from hunting with the Mendip) was as Clerk of the Peace for the City and County of Bristol, a position he held until it was abolished and he retired. When his chosen successor left the firm in 1966 I gradually became 'Jones the Transport' to differentiate me from 'Jones the Liquor' and 'Jones the Divorce', and the rest is history. When Peter Woodhouse replaced me he was only the third person in 75 years to lead the transport speciality in the firm, which in 2002 had merged with Bond Pearce.

Text footnotes

1 All Aboard 100 years of Trains, Trolleys and Buses in Cardiff – published by Cardiff Bus, South Wales Echo, Transbus International
2 The People's Carriage – Bristol Omnibus Company. Limited
3 Corpe on road haulage licensing' by T D Corpe OBE, revised by Elizabeth Havers and I R D Jenkins – Iliffe Books Ltd 1964
4 Standing Committee C, 8 May 1930
5 First Annual Report of the Traffic Commissioners
6 Published by Robson Books
7 Road Traffic Act 1930, section 62 and Parts 1 and 11 of Third Schedule
8 section 63
9 section 63(1)
10 10 section 98(3)
11 11 section 99
12 12 Select Committee C, 6 May 1930
13 13 ibid
14 14 section 63(5)
15 15 section 63(3)
16 16 section 63(6)
17 Committee stage, 1 May 1930
18 See Appendix 3
19 section 63(2)
20 section 63(10)
21 section 63(11)
22 Chairmen of Traffic Commissioners, etc (Tenure of Office) Act 1937 amending ss.63(5) and 98(5) of the 1930 Act.
23 Notes on Commissioners' Meeting – 21 January 1931
24 First Annual Report
25 Select Committee C, 6 May 1930
26 section 64(1)
27 section 67 (1)
28 section 71
29 section 72(1)
30 section 72(3)
31 section 72(4)
32 section 73
33 section 73(2)
34 section 76
35 section 67(2)
36 section 74
37 section 68
38 section 77
39 section 93(1) and (2)
40 section 8(2) Road and Rai1 Traffic Act 1933
41 First Annual Report
42 ibid
43 ibid
44 ibid
45 ibid
46 Petrie and Great Western Railway Company 1934 A11
47 Cox and Great Western Railway Company 1934 A56
48 1935 B33
49 1934 A5
50 section 57

51 See Appendix 3
52 section 117 Transport Act 1947
53 section 1
54 section 1 (1)(a)
55 section 1 (1)(f)
56 see section 41
57 section 39
58 section 59
59 section 52
60 section 53
61 section 63(1)
62 section 63(1) and (2), and section 64(1)
63 section 65
64 section 1(1)
65 section 3(1) and (4)
66 section 7 and 8
67 section 59(3)(a)
68 section 18
69 sections 43 and 44 section
70 section 39
71 sections 121 and 119
72 Reed & Sons v Bristol Co-operative Society Ltd., (1937) 25 T.C. 241
73 Section 1
74 section 60 onwards
75 Schedule 9
76 section 1
77 section 24(1)(a) and (b) and Schedule 7
78 sections 10(1) and section 19(3)
79 section 21
80 RHA Ltd v. A Cash and A McCall 1975 M 15
81 sections 2 and 8, and Schedule 2
82 section 1(1)(b)
83 section 12
84 section 1(1)(d) and section 13
85 section 7
86 section 7(3)(a) and (b)
87 section 7(4)
88 section 8
89 section 36
90 sections 19 to 22
91 section 23
92 section 52 and Schedule 4
93 section 31
94 section 4 Transport Act 1985 amending section 54 Public Passenger Vehicles Act 1981
95 Section 26(1)(a) and (b), (d)(1) and (ii)
96 section 1
97 sections 16 and 30-32
98 under section 26 Transport Act 1985
99 section 115 amending section 111 Transport Act 1985
100 A. M. Richardson t/a D. J. Travel Consultants
101 Annual Report of the Commissioners 2003-04

Appendices

Appendix 1

The original Traffic Areas

Northern Traffic Area	The counties of Northumberland, Cumberland, Durham and Westmoreland, part of Lancashire, part of North Riding and the County Boroughs of Newcastle-upon-Tyne, Tynemouth, Carlisle, Darlington, Gateshead, South Shields, Sunderland, West Hartlepool, Barrow-in-Furness, and Middlesborough
Yorkshire Traffic Area	The counties of York, the remainder of North Riding, West Riding and East Riding, part of Derbyshire and the County Boroughs of Kingston-upon-Hull, York, Barnsley, Bradford, Halifax, Dewsbury, Doncaster, Huddersfield, Leeds, Rotherham, Sheffield, and Wakefield.
North-Western Traffic Area	The counties of Montgomery, Merioneth, Carnarvon (sic), Anglesey, Denbigh, Flint, Chester and the remainder of Lancashire, part of Derbyshire and the County Boroughs of Birkenhead, Chester, Stockport, Wallasey, Blackburn, Blackpool, Bolton, Burnley, Bury, Liverpool, Manchester, Oldham, Preston, Rochdale, St. Helens, Salford, Southport, Warrington, and Wigan
West Midland Traffic Area	The counties of Hereford, Salop, Stafford, Warwick and Worcester and the county boroughs of Burton-upon-Trent, Smethwick, Stoke-on-Trent, Walsall, West Bromwich, Wolverhampton, Birmingham, Coventry, Dudley, and Worcester.

East Midland Traffic Area	The counties of Nottingham, Rutland Leicester, Northampton, Huntingdon, Bedford, most of Bucks, most of Derby, the Soke of Peterborough, parts of Lindsey/Kesteven/Holland, and the county boroughs of Nottingham, Grimsby, Lincoln, Leicester, Northampton, and Derby
Eastern Traffic Area	Counties of Norfolk, the Isle of Ely, Cambridge, East Suffolk, and West Suffolk, parts of Essex and Hertford, and the county boroughs of Great Yarmouth, Norwich, Ipswich and Southend-on-Sea.
South Wales Traffic Area	Counties of Pembroke, Cardigan, Carmarthen, Brecon, Glamorgan, and Monmouth, and the county boroughs of Cardiff, Merthyr Tydfil, Swansea, and Newport.
Western Traffic Area	Counties of Cornwall, Devon, Somerset, and Gloucester, and the County Boroughs of Exeter, Plymouth, Bath, Bristol, and Gloucester.
Southern Traffic Area	The Counties of Oxford, Berks, Wilts, Dorset, Southampton, the Isle of Wight, parts of Bucks and the county boroughs of Oxford, Reading, Bournemouth, Portsmouth, and Southampton.
South-Eastern Traffic Area	The counties of East and West Sussex, parts of Surrey and Kent, and the county boroughs of Brighton, Eastbourne, Hastings, and Canterbury
Metropolitan Traffic Area	The Metropolitan Police District and the City of London
(Scottish) Northern Traffice Area	Counties of Caithness, Sutherland, Ross and Cromarty, Inverness, Nairn, Moray, Banff, Aberdeen, Orkney, Zetland, Clackmannan, Kinross, and Fife
(Scottish) Southern Traffic Area	The counties of Argyl, Stirling, Dumbarton, Renfrew, Lanark, Ayr, Wigtown, Kirkcudbright, Bute, Westlothian, Midlothian, East Lothian, Berwick, Peebles, Selkirk, Dumfries, and Roxburgh.

Appendix 2

Chronological listing of Traffic Commissioners

(See Appendix 3 for Regional Transport Commissioners 1940-1946)

Northern Scotland Traffic Area (1931-1939)
Sir John Maxwell, Kt., C.M.G., (01.01.31 to 08.03.32)
Henry Riches O.B.E (09.03.32 to //.//.//)

Southern Scotland Traffic Area (1931-1938)
Archibald Henderson

Southern Traffic Area (1931-1933)
Major-General Sir R. Ford, K.C.M.G., C.B., D.S.O., M.Inst. T.

Northern Traffic Area (1931-1985)
Henry Riches (01.01.1931 to 08.03.1932)
Sir John Maxwell, Kt., C.M.G. (09.03.1932 to ?)
Samuel W. Nelson, C.B.E, M.Inst.T. (//.//1949 to 03.10.1953)
John A. T. Hanlon, J.P. (01.11.1953 to 17.12.1975)
Bertram J. Forster, O.B.E., J.P., F.C.I.T. (18.12.1975 died January 1982)
Major-General V. H. J. (John) Carpenter C.B., M.B.E., F.C.I.T. (11.01.1982 to 1985)

Yorkshire Traffic Area (1931-1985)
Joseph Farndale (01.01. 1931 to ?)
Major F.S. Eastwood, C.B.E., M.Inst.T. (? to 30.11.1965)
H. E. Robson, M.A., F.C.I.T. (01.12.1965 to 31.01.1969)
Major-General Sir John Potter, K.B.E., C.B., F.C.I.T. (01.02.69 to 09.02.1973)
Randall S. Thornton M.A. (19.03.75 to 11.11.1975)
Major-General Sir V.H.J. Carpenter (see above) (//.//.1975 to 11.11.1985)

East Midland Traffic Area (1931-1985)
J. H. Stirk J.P., M.Inst.T. (01.01.1931 to 1946)
J.W. Fletcher (01.01.1947 to 02.12.1953)
A.G. Curtis O.B.E, M.Inst.T. (03.12.1953 to //.//.1959)
C.P. Hodgson O.B.E., F.C.I.T. (//.//.1959 to 24.02.65)
C.M. Sheridan C.M.G., P.M.N. (25.02.1965 to //.12.1981)
Kenneth Peter, B.A., F.C.I.T. (//.12.1981 to //.//.1985)

Metropolitan Traffic Area (1931-1993)
Gleeson E. Robinson. M.C., LL.B. (01.01.1931 to ?)
Brigadier R J. O. Douse, C.B.E., M.I.Mech.E., M.Inst.T. (?-1959/60)
B.I.R. Muir (1959/60 to 11.02.1973)
A.S. Robertson, M.A. F.C.I.T. (12.02.1973 to //.8.1985)
Air Vice Marshal Ronald G. Ashford, C.B.E., LL.B. (//.08.1985 to //.//.1993)

West Midland Traffic Area
Colonel A.S. Redman, C.B., M.Inst.T. (01.01.1931 to 31.12.1937)
H. Trevor Morgan. M.C., K.C., M.A., LL.B. (01.01.1938 to ?)

R Stuart Pilcher, C.B.E, F.R.S.E., M.Inst.T. R.E. (? to 27.01.1952)
W.P. James. O.B.E. (28.01.1952 to 28.02.1961)
John Else (01.03.1961 to 31.07.1972)
Ronald R. Jackson. F.C.I.T., A.I.T.A., Hon F.I.R.T.E (01.08.1972 to 31.03.1974)
Arthur A. Crabtree. LL.B., D.P.A., T.D., F.C.I.T. (01.04.1974 to 15.04.1983)
Ronald R. Jackson (see above) (18.04.1983 to //.06.1986)
John Mervyn C. Pugh (//.06.1986 to 18.05.1998)
David Dixon. F.C.I.L.T. (19.05.1998 to date)

North-Western Traffic Area
W. Chamberlain, M.Inst.T. (01.01.1931 to ?)
F. Williamson, O.B.E., M.Inst.T. (28.10.48 to 28.02.1962)
Major-General A.F. J. (Fred) Elmslie, C.B., C.B.E., F.I.Mech.E., F.C.I.T. (01.03.1962 to 24.02-1965) (born 31.10.1905 died 13.09.2005)
Charles R. Hodgson, O.B.E., F.C.I.T. (25.02.1965 to 24.01.1975)
R. D. Hutchings, F.C.I.T. (25.01.1975 died 09.04.1987)
Keith R. Waterworth (//.04.1987 to //.10.1987)
Martin S. Albu (26.10.1987 to 31.12.1995)
Keith R. Waterworth (01.01.1996 to //.11.1999)
Beverley Bell (//.04.2000 to date)

Eastern Traffic Area.
Sir E. Haviland Hiley. K.B.E. (01.01.1931 to ?)
Sir Alfred Faulkner, C.B., C.B.E, M.Inst.T. (? To 18.10.51)
W. P. S. Ormond, M.A., M.Inst.T. (19.10.51 to 31.01.69)
H. E. Robson, M.A., M.Inst.T. (01.02.1969 to 30.06.1977)
Kenneth Peter, B.A., F.C.I.T. (01.07.1977 to 11.05.1986)
John Mervyn C Pugh (11.05.1986 to 11.02.1987)
Brigadier Compton M Boyd (//.02.1987 to 15.06.1998)
Geoffrey Simms (16.06.1998 to date)

South Wales Traffic Area (and Wales Traffic Area).
A. T. James, K.C., J.P. (01.01.1931 to ?)
H. J. Thom, C.I.E., M.C., M.A., M.Inst.T (? to 17.11.1953)
C.R. Hodgson, O.B.E., F.C.I.T. (18.11.53 to 11.11.1959)
I. I. Owen (//.//.1959 to 30.09.1961)
C. R. Hodgson (see above) (01.10.61 to 05.11.61)
Ronald R. Jackson (06.11.1961 to //.//.1986)
John Mervyn C. Pugh (//.//.1986 to 18.05.1998)
David Dixon, F.C.I.L.T. (19.05.1998 to date).

Western Traffic Area.
A. F. Nicholson, O.B.E. (01.01.1931 to ?)
Sir Arnold Musto, C.I.E., M.I.C.E. (? To 31.10.1953)
Stanley W. Nelson. C.B.E., M.Inst.T. (04.10.1953 to 25.05.1964)
J. R. C. Samuel-Gibbon (25.05.64 to 09.02.1973)
Major-General Sir John Potter (see above) (12.02.1973 to 15.04.1983)
Arthur A. Crabtree (see above) (18.04.1983 to 11.09.1984)

Ronald R. Jackson (see above) (//.09.1984 to ?)
Major General S. J. V. Carpenter (see above) (1985 to 1991)
Air Vice Marshal Ronald Ashford (see above) (1991 to 11.05.1996)
John Mervyn C. Pugh (11.05.1996 to 06.01.1997)
Christopher S. Heaps, LL.B., F.C.I.L.T. (07.01.1997 to //.05.2000)
Philip Brown (//.05.2000 to date)

South Eastern Traffic Area (South Eastern and Metropolitan Traffic Area)
Rowland Harker, K.C. (0.01.1931 to ?1934)
Sir Henry H. Piggott, C.B., C.B.E. (1934 to 31.12.1946)
Brigadier R. J. O. Dowse, C.B.E., M.I.Mech.E., M.Inst.T. (01.01.1947-?)
Lieutenant Colonel F. Gordon Tucker, O.B.E., T.D. (? to 17.11.1953)
G. J. Thom, C.I.E., M.C., M.A., M.Inst.T. (18.11.1953 to 22.04.1965)
Major-General A. F. J. Elmslie (see above) (25.02.1965 to 11.11.1975)
Randall S. Thornton, M.A. (11.11.1975 to 31.08.1986)
Brigadier M. H. Turner, LL.B., M.C.I.T. (01.09.1986 to 31.12.1999)
Christopher S. Heaps (see above) (04.01.2000 to date)

North Eastern Traffic Area. (1985 to date)
Fred Whalley, C.Eng., M.I.Mech.E., F.C.I.T., M.I.R.T.E. (1985 to 1993)
Keith R. Waterworth (see above) (//.//.1993 to 28.02.200)
Brigadier Tom Macartney (01.03.2000 to date)

Scottish Traffic Area (1962 to date)
W. F. Quinn, J.P., M.Inst.T. (1962 to 1964)
A. B. (Sandy) Birnie (to 1979)
Hugh McNamara (1980 to 1990)
Keith Waterworth (1990 to 1993)
Michael Betts, C.B.E., F.C.I.L.T. (1993 to 2002)
Joan Aitken (2003 to date)

Appendix 3

Regional Transport Commissioners

(Commissioners pre-War *, in post 1946**)

1940

North Western:	Mr W Chamberlain*
Wales:	Mr A T James*
Metropolitan:	Gleeson E Robinson*
Southern:	Sir Henry H Piggott*
North Eastern:	Maj. F S Eastwood*/**
Scotland:	Archibald Henderson*/**
Eastern:	Sir E Haviland Hiley*/**
Northern:	Sir John Maxwell*/**
South Western:	H. Trevor Morgan*/**
N Scotland:	Henry Riches*
North Midland:	Mr J H Stirk*/**
South Eastern:	Lt-Col F Gordon Tucker
North Wales:	Mr T D Jones

1941

North Western:	Chamberlain
Wales:	James
Metropolitan:	Robinson
Southern:	Piggott
North Eastern:	Eastwood
Scotland:	Henderson
Eastern:	Hiley
Northern:	Maxwell
South Western:	Morgan
Midland:	Sir Arnold Musto
N Scotland:	Riches
North Midlands:	Stirk
South Eastern:	Tucker
North Wales:	Mr J R Williams

1942

North Western:	Chamberlain
North Wales:	Morgan
London:	Robinson
Southern:	Piggott
North Eastern:	Eastwood
Scotland:	Henderson
Eastern:	Hiley
Northern:	Maxwell
South Western:	Sir Alfred Robinson
South Western:	Musto
Midland:	Musto
North Midland:	Stirk

1943

North Western:	Chamberlain
Wales:	Morgan
North Wales	Williams
London:	Robinson
Southern:	Piggott
Scotland:	Henderson
Eastern:	Hiley
Northern:	Maxwell
South Western:	Henderson
South Western:	Stirk
South Eastern:	Tucker
South Eastern:	Tucker

1944

Northern:	Maxwell
North Eastern:	Eastwood
North Midland:	Stirk
Eastern:	Faulkner
London:	Robinson
Southern:	Piggott
South Western:	Robinson
Wales(Cardiff):	Morgan
Wales(Caernavon):	Williams
Midland:	Musto
North Western:	Chamberlain
Scotland:	Henderson
South Eastern:	Tucker

1945

Northern:	Maxwell
North Eastern:	Eastwood
North Midland:	Stirk
Eastern:	Faulkner
London:	Robinson
Southern:	Piggott
South Western:	A Robinson
Wales(Cardiff):	Morgan
Wales(Caernavon):	Williams
Midland:	Musto
North Western:	vacant
Scotland:	Henderson
South Eastern:	Tucker

1946

Northern:	Maxwell**
North Eastern:	Eastwood**
North Midland:	Stirk**
Eastern:	Faulkner**
London:	Robinson
Southern:	Piggott**
South Western:	Robinson
Wales Cardiff):	Morgan**
Wales Caernavon):	Williams
Midland:	Musto**
North Western:	Mr W E C Macue
Scotland:	Henderson**

Appendix 4

Profiles of Traffic Commissioners: then and now

Henry Riches: born in Norfolk. Ex-Chief Constable of Scarborough and Middlesborough. Instrumental in establishing the North Yorkshire and South Durham Regional Advisory Committee on Traffic Control for licensing bus services. Seconded to the Ministry of Transport to assist with the implementation of the RTA 1930. The first Commissioner to be appointed.

Joseph Farndale: born 6 April 1885. Former Chief Constable of Margate, York and Bradford.

W Chamberlain: born 1877. Employed by Lancaster and Wallasey Electricity Departments before Mersey Docks and Harbour Board. He transferred to Oldham becoming general manager of the tramways department in 1918. Subsequently general manager at Leeds and Belfast. Sometime President of the Municipal Tramways and Transport Association.

Colonel Arthur Stanley Redman: born 25 September 1879. An army career via Royal Indian Engineering College. Survey in the Orange River Colony 1905-8. Movement Director, War Office 1914-20. Traffic Superintendent Somerset and Dorset Railway 1920-1. Assistant Director of Movement, War Office 1921-4. Director of Transportation, War Office, 1924-5. Assistant Adjutant General 1926-30.

J H Stirk: Worked for the Midland Railway and then as manager of the Birmingham Co-operative Society transport department.

Sir Ernest Haviland Hiley: born June 1870. Joined the N. E. Railway in 1891, posts included Docks Manager at Hull and Newcastle. 1905-8 Passenger Manager G.N.R., 1913-19 General Manager New Zealand Government Railways (including service on New Zealand H.O. Staff). Member of Royal Commission on local Government of London 1921-3. Adviser on Rhodesian Railways 1925-6.

Abraham Thomas James: born 18 April 1883. Qualified as a solicitor 1904 (First in First Class Honours). Until 1911 partner in Morgan Bruce Nicholas and James. 1911 called to the Bar and practiced on the South Wales Circuit. Chairman of Carmarthen Quarter Sessions.

A. F. Nicholson: Deputy Chief Constable of the Bradford City Police and latterly Chief Constable of Exeter.

Major-General Sir Reginald Ford: born 7 December 1868. Joined the Royal Marines 1889. Transferred to ASC 1893. Mentioned in dispatches twice in Boer War with 5 clasps and DSO. Mentioned 8 times in dispatches 1914-18.

Rowand Harker: born 18 January 1879. Qualified as a solicitor 1900. Called to the bar 1905, Middle Temple. 1914-1918. DAAG to Judge Advocate General. K.C. 1926.

Gleeson Edward Robinson: Solicitor 1904-15. Royal Field Artillery 1915-19 in France (mentioned in dispatches, MC and bar) 1920 admitted as a barrister to Middle

Temple. 1920-25 Secretary to the Clearing Office (Enemy Debts). British Member of Anglo-German Mixed Arbitral Tribunal: Public Authorities and Legal Liability.

Archibald Henderson: born 15 January 1886, son of an innkeeper. Educated at Simpson's Academy, Edinburgh and London School Board, City of London College. Clerk in various London offices 1901-13. L.C.C. Tramways Department 1913-15. Trade Union Official 1915-31. Traffic Commissioner 1931-48.

Sir John Maxwell: born 6 August 1875. Solicitor (Scotland) 1899. Assistant District Commissioner, Gold Coast 1902. Travelling Commissioner 1905-7. Provisional Commissioner. Secretary for Native Affairs 1923 (At various times Governor(2), Colonial Secretary, Attorney-General, Solicitor-General.) Latterly Commissioner for Ashanti.

Philip Brown: LL.B., M.A.(Cantab), F.C.I.L.T. Born 1953. 1975-1992 a solicitor/legal adviser in the Magistrates' Court Service, latterly with responsibility for the management and administration of the Service in Cambridgeshire. Director of Legal Studies for Continuing Legal Education in the University of Cambridge, particularly concerned with training lawyers and law students in Eastern Europe. Part-time Deputy Traffic Commissioner 1990 to 2000. Specialist Editor (Road Traffic) JP Reports and Editor Wilkinson's Road Traffic Offences (2005). Appointed Traffic Commissioner for the Western Traffic Area May 2000 and Senior Traffic Commissioner March 2003.

Christopher Seymour Heaps: born 15 November 1942. LL.B., F.C.I.L.T., admitted as a solicitor 1967. Solicitor/partner Eversheds (formerly Jaques & Co/Jaques & Lewis) until 1996. Member of the Council of the Law Society 1985-97; Chairman Law Society's Planning and Environmental Law Committee 1988-91, 1995-96; Member Council on Tribunals 1991-97; Member of Transport Users Consultative Committee for London and Deputy Chairman London Regional Passengers Committee. Director, The UK Bus Driver of the Year Association Ltd. Author: London Transport Railways Album; Western Region in the 1960s; Southern Region Central Division; [Editor of] B.R. Diary 1968-1977. Appointed Western Traffic Commissioner from 1997 to 2000, then South Eastern Traffic and Metropolitan Commissioner from 2000.

David Dixon: born 1942. F.C.I.L.T. Educated at Rugby and University College, Oxford. Traffic Management trainee with London Midland Region from 1964 and subsequent posts included Assistant Station Manager (Guide Bridge, Manchester) and Area Manager at Kensington, Olympia. From 1976 Associated British Pods as Secretary to the Board, Docks Manager, Fleetwood and Director, Small Ports. Managing Director Isle of Man Steam Packet Company from 1986 to 1998. Appointed Traffic Commissioner for the West Midlands and South Wales (all Wales from April 1999) May 1998.

Geoffrey Simms: F.C.I.L.T., F.R.S.A. Road haulier by profession, latterly as managing director of Capel Express (Ipswich) Limited which he founded in 1969. Entered the industry in 1957 after leaving Woking Grammar School. Chairman, Eastern District, Road Haulage Association 1989-1991 and Chairman International Group 1994-1996. Member of the Transport Tribunal 1990-1998. Appointed Traffic Commissioner for the Eastern Traffic Area June 1998.

Brigadier Tom Macartney: F.C.I.L.T. HGV driving licence. After graduating from the Royal Military Academy Sandhurst, he joined the Royal Corps of Transport in which he spent 34 years. He had, inter alia, responsibility for the Ghurka Transport School and the Chinese Transport School. His final responsibility was for transport policy for the three services including the Defence School of Transport. He is also a qualified second class steam engine driver's mate. Appointed Traffic Commissioner for the North Eastern Traffic Area February 2000.

Beverley Bell: F.C.I.L.T., LL.B., Certificate of Professional Competence (National); admitted as a solicitor 1984 and practised criminal law and prosecuted for the Vehicle Inspectorate. Appointed Traffic Commissioner for the North Western Traffic Area April 2000 (first female full-time appointee).

Joan Aitken: F.C.I.L.T., solicitor and first woman to be admitted to the Society of Solicitors in the Supreme Court of Scotland; former member of the Council of the Law Society of Scotland and editor of its Journal; past part-time Chairman of Employment Tribunals, Disability Appeal Tribunals and Child Support Appeal Tribunals (Scotland); from 1999 to March 2003 Prison Complaints Commissioner (Ombudsman) for Scotland. Appointed Traffic Commissioner for the Scottish Traffic Area March 2003: lay member of the General Dental Council (Scotland).